I0032680

Governance and Social Leadership

Robert A. Campbell

CAPE BRETON UNIVERSITY PRESS
SYDNEY, NOVA SCOTIA

Copyright © 2014 Robert A. Campbell

All rights reserved. No part of this work may be reproduced or used in any form or by any means, electronic or mechanical, including photocopying, recording or any information storage or retrieval system, without the prior written permission of the publisher. Cape Breton University Press recognizes fair dealing uses under the *Copyright Act* (Canada). Responsibility for the research and permissions obtained for this publication rests with the author.

Cape Breton University Press recognizes the support of the Province of Nova Scotia, through the Department of Communities, Culture and Heritage and the support received for its publishing program from the Canada Council for the Arts Block Grants Program. We are pleased to work in partnership with these bodies to develop and promote our cultural resources.

FILM & CREATIVE INDUSTRIES NOVA SCOTIA

Canada Council   Conseil des Arts
for the Arts   du Canada

Cover image: Miami Night, by Erin MacKeen, Toronto, ON
Cover design: Cathy MacLean Design, Pleasant Bay, NS
Layout: Mike Hunter, Port Hawkesbury and Sydney, NS
First printed in Canada.
Second printing 2014

Library and Archives Canada Cataloguing in Publication

Campbell, Robert A. (Robert Arthur), 1952-, author
 Governance and social leadership / Robert A. Campbell.
Includes bibliographical references and index.

Issued in print and electronic formats.
ISBN 978-1-897009-70-3 (pbk.).-- ISBN 978-1-927492-64-2
(pdf).--ISBN 978-1-927492-65-9 (epub).--ISBN 978-1-927942-66-6
(mobi)

1. Leadership. 2. Leadership--Social aspects. I. Title.
HM1261.C34 2014 303.3'4 C2014-900508-3
C2014-900509-1

Cape Breton University Press
PO Box 5300, 1250 Grand Lake Road
Sydney, NS B1P 6L2 CA
www.cbupress.ca

Governance and Social Leadership

Table of Contents

List of Figures

Preface

The ideas expressed here reflect my personal struggles over the past few decades to understand governance and leadership. My experience working in industry and the nonprofit sectors combined with my academic background in sociology, both as a student and as a faculty member, have provided me with a great deal of exposure to a variety of manifestations and understandings of these phenomena. The net result of this exposure, however, has been an increasing frustration over how little we actually know about these critical areas of public concern and how often both are abused to facilitate the pursuit of personal interest.

The actual work of trying to articulate my position on these matters emerged out of my experience developing and teaching an advanced course on leadership for students in the MBA program in community economic development, for the Shannon School of Business at Cape Breton University, in Sydney, Nova Scotia. My use of the word advanced is meant to capture two things. First, students taking the course have already completed the core business courses, including courses in organizational behaviour, leadership and community economic development. Second, the course provides the opportunity to expose students to a theoretically more challenging exploration of issues related to governance and leadership—one that raises as many questions as answers, but also develops their skills in analysis and synthesis.

That being said, this is not a textbook. It does not attempt to provide a systematic and comprehensive coverage of leadership or governance in an objective and sterile manner, with specific learning goals, sidebars, illustrations, glossaries, questions for reflection and cases for review and application. Nor is it an academic monograph, grounded in a specific theoretical framework, following a particular methodology in an attempt to prove, or at least support, some hypothesis, through the collection and analysis of data. Similarly, it is not a trade book aimed at the presumed intelligent and interested general reader, written in a familiar, if not journalistic, style, providing enthusiastic, if not particularly deep, insight into some phenomenon of interest, anchored in current events, while keeping notes and references to a minimum. *Rather it has a bit of all three.* Because I am an academic, and because I am concerned that all readers understand the sources of my ideas and are provided with ample direction to pursue their own interests in a more systematic and informed manner, it is somewhat pedantic in its method of presentation. At the same time, I hope that I have managed to write it in a manner that will appeal, and be of some use, to students, academics, practitioners and the general reader. More than anything else, however, it is a guidebook based on my own journey toward understanding the relationship between leadership and governance and developing the notion of social leadership.

Governance and leadership are distinct but inseparable aspects of organizational life. Regrettably, the concept of leadership has been overused to the extent of rendering it almost meaningless. Governance, most often equated with government, is well on its way to suffering the same fate. Despite our misunderstanding of these concepts, governance structures provide the environment in which leadership can emerge. The idea of social leadership captures two critical elements beyond this. First, it draws attention to the fact that the process of carrying out leadership must be one that is social. In other words, it must involve constructive interaction among those involved. Second, the product of the exercise of leadership must be social. It must contribute to social wellbeing in a substantial and sustainable way.

I want to thank the many students who have taken leadership courses from me over the last couple of decades, both in university classrooms and in other venues, for allowing me to subject them to various experiments in pedagogy, course content and ways of thinking. Thanks also to Brittany Erickson, Catherine Leviten-Reid, Jacke Scott and Janice Tulk for their helpful comments and suggestions throughout the writing process.

Robert Campbell, Sydney, Nova Scotia, May 2014

1. Setting the Stage

B riefly stated, there are three reasons for you to read this book. First, rather than providing another theory of leadership, I am offering a new model of how to understand leadership—one that hinges on a particular interpretation of the word social. Second, I dare to explore not just one of the most overused and least understood concepts in the organizational studies vocabulary (leadership), I also tackle the increasingly used but equally misunderstood concept of governance. Third, I am making a deliberate effort to be troublesome.

One of the ways that I mean to be troublesome is through the introduction of disparate ideas from a variety of academic disciplines (arts, humanities, natural and social sciences) and realms of experience (family, school, work, play and community), many of which are not frequently used in discussions of leadership. Some of these ideas should immediately seem germane to the subject matter at hand, while others may appear to be trivial or superfluous. I learned long ago not to underestimate the power of anecdote as an aid to understanding (see Solway 1991); I prefer to interpret "trivial" in the outdated scholastic sense of foundational, rather than in the newer unfortunate sense of superfluous, or irrelevant.

My approach to studying ideas is consistent with what Johns Hopkins University historian Arthur O. Lovejoy (1873-1962) referred to as the history of ideas (1960). This field is exemplified

1

by interdisciplinary research projects for which the proper unit of analysis is the idea and the appropriate task for the researcher is to discover the origins, modes of expression, means of preservation and manifold changes that these ideas undergo through time. Similarly, my approach is influenced by what philosopher Alfred North Whitehead (1861-1947) called the adventure of ideas (1967). Not only was Whitehead interested in examining those ideas that came to form the intellectual foundation of Western civilization, he also used this expression to imply an attitude of adventure and play—one in which the researcher is always open to, and indeed should purposefully attempt to find, novel ways of thinking about things.

My approach can also be viewed as being genealogical, in two senses of that word. The first sense, which is similar to the way it is used in regard to the increasingly popular pastime of tracing one's family tree, can be captured by the declaration that, "if I have seen further, it is because I have stood on the shoulders of giants." This well-rehearsed saying, used primarily by those engaged in what are commonly referred to as the hard sciences, is of course a metaphor for making progress by building on the work of those who came before you. In the form it is stated here it is attributed to the mathematician and physicist Isaac Newton (1642-1727), but it appears in the first instance to have been used by the 12th-century philosopher Bernard of Chartres (d. 1130), in reference to the lasting legacy of ancient Greek thinkers. It is not the implied modesty contained in this statement, even when false, that concerns me, but rather the path of indebtedness that it acknowledges. If you are going to rely on what others have done before you, and you really have no choice but to do so, then you should at least have a rudimentary awareness of who those others were, and how they came to define and dominate a particular discourse.

The second sense of "genealogical" might appear to contradict the first. In an effort to trace the origins of his own thought processes, French philosopher Michel Foucault (1926-1984) wrote a brilliant essay entitled, "Nietzsche, genealogy, history." In this essay, which became the first chapter of his *The Archaeology of Knowledge* (1972), he suggests that genealogy is not the search for the origins of an idea, or the attempt to construct a distinct path of linear development. Rather, it is the task of discovering the pluralistic and often contradictory threads that come together to contribute to our understanding of ideas, as a means of exposing the influence that power has had on the construction of truth. Foucault was interested in uncovering irregularities and inconsistencies; in a way, his genealogies say more about those who construct an idea, and their reasons for doing so, than they do about the idea itself. I prefer to see the two senses as complementary.

As an initial example of a concept that normally does not enter into discussions of leadership, in the late 1950s, psychiatrist and pioneer in the field of cybernetics, Ross Ashby (1903-1972), formulated the Law of Requisite Variety. Stated in its bluntest form, this law says that, "only variety can destroy variety" (Ashby 2011: 206). Ashby was concerned with the problem of regulating complex systems, particularly missile guidance systems, but also with applications like the creation of effective broad-spectrum antibiotics. His ideas were influenced by developments in information theory, especially those of the field's major pioneer, Claude Shannon (1916-2001), who was concerned with the fact that too much information increases the uncertainty of properly understanding a message (1948). However, Ashby's notion of requisite variety entails both quantitative (how much variety) and qualitative (what kind of variety) components. He recognized that part of understanding and potentially controlling a system required accounting for the heterogeneity among the parts that make up a system, the diverse sets of connections that may exist between these parts, and the types of interactions that might take place between these parts.

Helmut Nechansky (2008) restates Ashby's law in the negative form: if a system does not possess the requisite variety, it will be unable to cope with the challenges it faces. For our purposes then, this law implies that if our understanding of leadership is not as complex as the leadership situations that we will encounter, we will not be able to deal with those situations effectively. This observation gives rise to a number of questions, of which the most obvious is likely to be one of how we produce leaders with requisite variety. One potential response is to look at the possibility of distributing understanding among a number of individuals, thereby establishing a more responsive system by tapping into collective intelligence. Of course, the problem then becomes one of how to organize in such a way as to facilitate collective action. Attempting to resolve this latter issue is central to the development of the concept of social leadership and, I would suggest, the effective management of complex human systems is, of necessity, predicated on the constructive entanglement of modes of leadership and modes of governance.

Threshold Concepts

The second way I try to be troublesome is through the presentation of ideas, some of which I hope will prove to be threshold concepts for many readers. In a series of articles beginning in 2003, Jan Meyer and Ray Land develop the notion of threshold concepts in higher education. These are concepts that are specific to the knowledge base and nomenclature of a particular discipline or realm of human activity, which possess the following four characteristics: they are transformative, integrative, irreversible—and troublesome. When an idea has the effect of bringing about a change in perception or practice, then it is transformative. If that idea leads to an awareness of patterns and connections within a body of knowledge, then it is integrative. To categorize an idea as irreversible means that it is something that you will not likely be able to forget or unlearn. Finally, a troublesome notion is one that may be counter-intuitive; more importantly, it is definitely going to be unsettling, or disorienting, leading to the development of a reconstitutive change in understanding or practice.

Many years ago, I was having a discussion with a co-worker about the value of acquiring a basic understanding of physics. He told me that when he was taking physics in high school, his instructor had said that the only reason he appeared to be standing still was because the floor was pushing up on him with the same amount of force that he was pushing down on the floor. My co-worker was convinced that this counter-intuitive notion was a convenient fiction, created by and for physicists, but not actually a characteristic of the physical world. While Newton's Third Law of Motion, the particular bit of physics in question here, may appear trivial, or something you could happily live the rest of your life without knowing, I provide this example, in part to stress the final characteristic of threshold concepts—the fact that they are troublesome. Troublesome concepts can be quite threatening, and as with other threats, denial or avoidance are common and convenient defense mechanisms.

Certainly, as anyone who has learned something new can attest, acquiring knowledge, especially when it involves questioning what we already know, requires a period of discomfort, disorientation and, often, denial. Pedagogically, there is an onus on the teacher/mentor/leader to provide an environment in which this liminality (sense of disorientation, in-between-ness) can be resolved. Otherwise, the comfort of ignorance may trump the liberating effect of knowledge. Of course, this same process has the effect of separating out the next generation of physicists from those destined to pursue other interests. Lack of ability or desire can unhinge the best of intentions.

Researchers have identified a number of threshold concepts in business-related fields, including the ideas of depreciation in accounting (Lucas and Mladenovic 2006) and opportunity cost in economics (Meyer and Land 2003). With respect to threshold concepts in leadership, on the basis of participant observation in a leadership class, Jeffrey Yip and Joseph Raelin (2011) found that two ideas stood out: situational leadership and shared leadership. Learning the former concept, initially developed by Paul Hersey and Ken Blanchard (1967), had the effect of leading to an appreciation of the contextual aspects of leadership. Understanding the latter concept, which reflects a broad set of approaches rather than a specific theory (see Raelin 2003), caused a shift from the more independent, egocentric conception of leadership prevalent among the students to one that encompasses interdependence and broader participation. As we proceed, recognizing the importance of context and interdependence is critical to understanding the concept of social leadership. At the same time, I cannot identify what, if anything, I have to say in these pages will constitute a threshold concept for any particular reader. All I can do is provoke. Hopefully the effort will not be interpreted as provocation for its own sake.

Building on this latter point, being troublesome can also be viewed as a form of what ethnomethodologist Harold Garfinkel (1917-2011) referred to as a breaching experiment (1967). Ethnomethodology is a mode of sociological inquiry that examines the everyday methods that people use to create social order. We all develop patterns of behaviour—as individuals and in concert with others—which we use to establish and maintain a sense of normalcy in our lives. These patterns become second nature to the extent that we are often no longer aware of what it is that we do. A breaching experiment is one in which routine activities are purposefully disrupted in order to observe and identify those elements that constitute the normative pattern.

Some years ago I was asked to direct a seminar for a group of teachers who were working toward an advanced education certificate while on sabbatical from their classrooms. I thought long and hard about how to go about this exercise in order to derive maximum benefit from the short time that we had together, mindful of the fact that these individuals had been teaching for twenty-five years. I chose David Solway's book, *Lying about the Wolf* (1997), as the focus for our discussions, and for the first meeting I asked them to read just the first two pages. As an opening remark, I announced that I was going to demonstrate to them that they did not know how to read, or at least, even if they had once known how, that over the years they had forgotten how. Amidst the anticipated skepticism and thinly veiled hostility generated by this insult, I spent the next two hours going through those two pages word-by-word, phrase-by-phrase, sentence-by-sentence and paragraph-by-paragraph, until they had convinced themselves that perhaps their reading skills could use a bit of work.

There are two points to make here. First, it is possible, and I would suggest relatively common in human experience, that the troublesome aspect of a concept precedes the opportunity for it to be transformative, integrative or irreversible. In *Gulliver's Travels* (1726), a satirical novel by Jonathan Swift (1667-1745), a Balnibarbian architect devises a scheme for building houses from the roof down (see Solway 1997: 41-67). It seems to me that all too often this is exactly how governance and leadership—in fact, all forms of management—are practiced and experienced. Thus, to my second point, the pedagogical and leadership opportunity in many instances may be one of going back to help people build the house upon which that roof is perched.

∞∞∞∞

Turning now to the second reason for you to read this book, as reflected in the book's title, I am writing not only about leadership, but also about governance. This approach is not original to me either. Rather, it is consistent with an emerging, but as yet highly underdeveloped, trend in organizational management studies (see Erakovic and Jackson 2009). To some extent this trend is growing in response to the recognition of the importance of context in understanding and practicing leadership and governance. At the same time it can be seen as a response to the growing public disillusionment and anxiety in the presence of so many failures of our present leadership and governance systems. Among other things, these failures highlight the inadequacy of our current theories to help us understand what actually takes place in these arenas and to suggest mechanisms for correction. One of the first points of clarification necessary for the constructive integration of these two concepts is that governance is not equivalent to government. These ideas are explored in greater depth in the coming chapters.

The primary reason for you to read this book, though, is because I am presenting a new model of how to think about leadership. While the exact details of this model are not spelled out until the final chapter, all of the pieces necessary for final assembly will be introduced throughout. The key distinction to be made at this point is that when I use the words leader and leadership, I will be using them in a very general sense that encompasses the vast array of meanings they have acquired among academics, leadership gurus, media pundits and the general public. As an extension of this use, I will sometimes be implying something a bit more judgmental, along the lines of what Maltese physician, and Da Vinci Professor of Thinking at the University of Advancing Technology, Edward de Bono (b. 1933) called porridge words— words that are very useful but meaningless (1971). When I use the term social leadership, I am referring directly to my own model.

Some might suggest that there is a level of redundancy in using the expression social leadership, because all leadership is social. They may argue that there can be no such thing as non-social leadership, and perhaps they are right. However, I think it is safe to suggest that there are forms of asocial leadership—leadership that ignores or disregards the human component—and we know very well that there are forms of anti-social leadership aimed at undermining or negating the human element. Consequently, at a minimum, the expression social leadership is useful with respect to making these sorts of distinctions. As you might expect, however, I am using the word social in a particular way, and thus its use to modify the word leadership takes on particular significance in what follows.

As a cautionary note before moving on, let me reiterate that my model is not a new *theory* of leadership, but rather a *model* for understanding leadership—a heuristic tool to be used to identify assumptions about leadership. But, beyond that, and more prescriptively, it is also a model of what leadership theories and practice should be.

The Academic Study of Leadership

Anticipating another source of apprehension, I acknowledge that there are those who would likely contend that the academic study of leadership is too far removed from the actual practice of leadership. While this sort of criticism could be levelled at any and every academic discipline, it takes on special significance with respect to leadership. In part, this is because we continue to witness so much bad leadership on the part of politicians, corporate executives and religious leaders—to name a few. As a consequence, we are particularly skeptical about ivory-tower proclamations and the ramblings of gurus and pundits, all the while being desperate for insight.

Of course, you do not need to be familiar with the details of any particular theory of leadership in order to be an effective leader. Like the *bourgeois gentilhomme*, title character in the play (1670) by French playwright Molière (1622-1673), who was astonished to learn that he had been speaking prose his whole life without knowing it, you may be performing as an exemplary transformational leader, without knowing there was a name for it. However, as you watch others attempt to lead, or as you try to improve your own leadership skills, knowing something about the way in which leadership theories are constructed and categorized can help you not only to identify leadership when it takes place, but also provide you with a means to analyze and evaluate its effectiveness.

On the assumption that leadership is something that can be taught, standard course texts on the subject (see Daft 2011; Yukl 2013) attempt to treat leadership in a systematic manner that reflects the best evidence available from research projects and case studies, all the while cautioning against the acceptance of ideas that have yet to be subjected to adequate empirical justification. Standalone textbooks on leadership are a relatively recent phenomenon, having evolved out of the subject matter usually covered in courses in organizational behaviour, or in what simply used to be called management. If you examine management textbooks from a few decades ago (see Donnelly et al. 1971; Hitt et al. 1986), not only will you find coverage of a similar suite of topics, you will also find that our assessment of the state of our knowledge on the subject is far from what we would like it to be. For example, the opening sentence in their chapter on leadership states: "Managerial scholars and practitioners have been perplexed for years by the phenomenon of leadership in organizations" (Donnelly et al. 1971: 185). Similarly, with respect to identifying the phenomenon to be studied, Hitt et al. are far more prescriptive, when they suggest that leadership has three major components: leaders must have followers, they must have the power to influence and that influence must be directed toward the accomplishment of goals (1986: 343). All three of these suppositions will be challenged in the pages that follow.

Of course, a more extensive and far more varied source of ideas and practical advice on leadership is to be found in the plethora of trade publications by business gurus and others who offer life lessons or yet another formula for success. A search on Amazon for books with the word leadership in the title (late 2013) returned more than 40,000 items. These books, and the multimedia support materials that often accompany them, play into our need for quick fixes and novelty, but they also demonstrate how little we really understand. I am not suggesting that these sources have nothing to offer. In fact, I would suggest that we often gain our greatest insights into almost any subject from the most unlikely of sources. The point I am trying to make is that our understanding of leadership is always partial and changing, and that any contribution to our understanding, irrespective of its form or content, is going to be fractional at best.

Academically, I take a sociological approach to the study of leadership. Sociology can be defined in several ways, but the critical elements to keep in mind as we proceed are that the focus is on the activities that people engage in collectively rather than as individuals, and the key questions to be answered have to do with how social order is established and maintained and how social change takes place. These questions can be posed in many different ways and there is a wide array of approaches to answering them that all could be considered sociological. While I would not claim to adhere strictly to any one theoretical or methodological framework within sociology, my perspective can be viewed as reflecting social constructionism, symbolic interactionism, phenomenology, economic sociology and the sociology of language, among others. These labels may be of no concern to the majority of readers, but they are useful to the extent that they indicate the kinds of sources being referred to, the vocabulary used and the reason I give preference to certain ideas over others.

Having said that, one of the major challenges with studying leadership, that only becomes more complicated when governance is added to the discussion, is that these concepts are a central component in the research agendas of scholars in anthropology, cultural studies, economics, management studies, political science, psychology, public administration, sociology and probably a few others. As you might anticipate, parallel lines of thought develop across these disciplines, and while it is an almost insurmountable task to keep up to date with all of the literature generated within one's own discipline, the thought of trying to maintain even a passing familiarity with what is going on in other disciplines is daunting. Consequently, some readers might come to wonder how I could possibly claim to be addressing key issues in leadership and governance without mentioning particular authors or ideas with which they are familiar, or in which they place great stock. There is likely no adequate response to this critique beyond acknowledging this situation as an occupational hazard—and a risk worth taking

My perspective as an academic researcher and teacher is balanced with several years of experience serving as a senior administrator at post-secondary institutions, working in industry and participating at various levels, both with respect to position and jurisdiction, in the so-called third (voluntary) sector. In all of these settings I witnessed a few examples of what I would identify as good leadership and altogether too many examples of what, in my view, was bad leadership. Some of what made these occurrences good or bad had to do with individual leaders, but in many cases it had to do with the behaviour of followers or the circumstances under which all of those involved had to operate.

Chapter Outline

The ideas developed throughout this book are predicated on the assumption that your quest to understand leadership, irrespective of your purpose for doing so, will continue. Even a cursory glance at current events illustrates that our understandings and expectations about governance and leadership are constantly challenged by what actually goes on in the world. What I set out to do here is provide a framework within which to understand what is happening at the intersection of governance and leadership, through the lens of what I refer to as social leadership, and in a way that reflects my own struggles to understand these phenomena. It has been a tumultuous and, all too often, remarkably frustrating experience. I sometimes think that I would like to stop thinking about governance and leadership altogether, but I seem compelled to do otherwise.

Because this book documents a sort of voyage of discovery, the chapters that follow are meant to be read in order, each building upon what has come before. The specific subject matter of each chapter moves back and forth between issues more directly associated with leadership and issues of governance, in a pattern that I feel is logical, and which mirrors my own thought processes, more than it does any other guiding principle. While wending their way along this seemingly serpentine path, readers will observe that coverage of certain topics occurs more than once. My objective in these cases is reiteration and elaboration.

To establish a firm foundation for what follows, as well as demonstrate what constitutes a good foundation for understanding anything at all, Chapter 2 provides a brief introduction to some philosophical principles that can be used to categorize our ways of viewing the world. While this discussion betrays a bias toward the origins and developments of the Western intellectual tradition, such tradition provides the context in which the vast majority of debates over issues related to governance and leadership take place globally.

The third chapter begins to outline the particulars of my understanding of the word social by describing what it means to take a relational perspective on what is going on in the world. This includes an exploration of a key conceptual dichotomy from sociological theory; namely, the relationship between structure and agency. While these two phenomena have often been viewed in opposition to one another, more recent analyses have started to see them as working in combination to pattern social action

Chapter 4 introduces the idea of the capacity to act, by looking at the questions of what governance and leadership are for and where they take place. The main premise of this chapter, and indeed for the entire book, is that the whole rationale for the development and adoption of systems of governance and leadership is one of building capacity to carry out whatever objectives a social group has set for itself. Key to understanding the ways in which we organize ourselves for action is developing an appreciation of the important role of context and complexity.

Chapter 5 deals with the problem of resource allocation through an exploration of the concept of property rights and, more specifically, through a discussion of the notions of a commons and an anticommons. Somewhere between the extremes of unfettered access for all and total private control is a socially viable notion of optimal use.

Chapter 6 extends the discussion of context in the direction of the smaller-scale activity of meetings. On a basic level, the practice of various numbers of people gathering together to talk and share ideas and experiences is the most fundamental of social activities and is part of every aspect of our lives. Despite the fact that we spend so much time meeting with others, they are a source of constant frustration and it is unclear what, if anything, they accomplish.

Chapters 7 and 8 offer a review of some of the many ways in which people have tried to understand and describe leadership. Coverage of the material moves from differentiating between management and leadership, through an exploration of the ways in which leadership is taught, to explore the ways in which academics have carried out research and developed theories about leadership.

The next two chapters, 9 and 10, begin with the problem of defining governance, and move on to discussions of policy governance and global governance. The next sections contain an exploration of the three most common forms of organizational governance: namely, hierarchical, market and network governance. The final section introduces the concept of sustainability governance, which is viewed as distinct from the more familiar concept of sustainable governance.

The final two chapters draw together the various threads developed throughout and present the details of the social leadership model. Chapter 11 presents the notion of servant leadership, as developed by Robert Greenleaf and Max DePree. While in many respects the servant leadership model comes closest to my ideal of social leadership, there are prior developments within the broader areas of management and organizational studies that are predicated on some notion of the social, and thus might be viewed as precursors to the ideas developed here. Consequently, Chapter 12 begins with a survey of initiatives such as corporate social responsibility, social marketing and social entrepreneurship. The remainder of the chapter provides an elaboration of social leadership, clarifying its role as a heuristic device for understanding and evaluating theories of governance and leadership and reiterating the fact that it is not in itself a new theory of leadership, but rather a prescription for what leadership theories and practice should be.

2. Foundations

Along with a propensity for pedantry alluded to in the previous chapter, students and colleagues have in the past remarked that I have a bit of a preoccupation with words, as well as a decided bias towards classification schemes. My fascination with words has two aspects. First of all, I always want to know what things are called. Of course, just because you know the name for something does not mean that you understand what it is, which leads to the second aspect. When someone uses a particular word for something, do I, or do they, really know what they mean by that word? Precision in naming and the attribution of meaning are highly contested concepts, but I think it is fair to suggest that the establishment of a common vocabulary with some rudimentary form of common understanding makes discussions about any topic more productive.

As for classification schemes, like words, they are useful to the extent that they facilitate discussion and the development of understanding. The objective in using them is not to provide a definitive categorization of the phenomena that we encounter. In this regard, and consistent with what Thomas Kuhn (1922-1996) decades ago pointed out about paradigms in scientific research (1970), I would suggest that, often in the face of challenges, it is probably a better idea to devote intellectual resources to the creation of a new classification scheme, than it is to attempt to force outliers and anomalies into existing systems. After all, as the pre-Socratic philosopher Heraclitus (535-475 BCE) stated twenty-five centuries ago, change is the only constant.

In what follows, four domains of philosophical inquiry are introduced that describe different aspects of the way we view the world. They are: ontology, epistemology, axiology and nomology. We owe the terminology and initial formulation of these concepts to the ancient Greeks, most prominently, Plato (427-347 BCE) and Aristotle (384-322 BCE). At a popular level, Plato is remembered for having introduced the world to Socrates (469-399 BCE), famous for his method of teaching through questioning, while Aristotle—a student of Plato's—was the private tutor of Alexander the Great (356-323 BCE), famous for having conquered most of what is now Europe, the Middle East and North Africa, all before the age of thirty-three. Within the context of philosophy, Plato thought in terms of intangible forms (every chair is an imperfect representation of ideal chair-ness), while Aristotle focused on concrete substances (the only chair worth considering is one you can sit in). As previously stated when discussing genealogy, the influence of ancient Greek thought on our current thought processes cannot be overestimated.

Returning to the four terms, the suffix for each one, from the word *logos* (meaning word), refers to the formal study of some thing or other. The four specific subjects of study, as reflected in the corresponding prefixes, are: being (*ontos*), knowledge (*episteme*), value (*axia*) and rules (*nomos*). Your world view may be more elaborate than can be adequately described by these four alone, but at the very least it will include these four. One of the key justifications for starting our deliberations with coverage of these topics is that our position with respect to these aspects of our world view is often taken for granted. What is more, not only are we often unaware of what our ontology, for example, may be, many of us are not even aware that we have something called an ontology.

Existence and Causality

Ontology is the study of what is—what sorts of entities constitute the world and how are these entities related to one another? Responses to these kinds of questions are rightly viewed as forming the most fundamental aspect of our thought systems and ways of viewing of the world. At the same time, there are some people who would likely contend that this sounds like the ultimate form of navel gazing, preferring to get on with their lives in the world as given. Would that it were that easy! At a very practical level, ontologies provide us with a sense of causality—a position regarding what sorts of things can make something happen, and how they do so.

Margaret Stout provides an ontological primer for researchers and practitioners in public administration, stating that, "identifying the underlying ontological assumptions of administrative theory is critical not only to understand and evaluate legitimacy claims in public administration, but to establish normative goals for practice" (2012a: 391-92). She describes the critical elements that constitute alternate ontological frameworks through the articulation of a series of dichotomies. First, existence is either static or dynamic. The latter perspective is reflected in Heraclitus' notion that change is the only constant. This view is contrasted with that of another pre-Socratic philosopher, Parmenides (fl. early 5th century BCE), who taught that reality was static, and that change was merely an illusion. Second, existence is either unitary and whole, or plural. This dichotomy is sometimes expressed through the debate about whether there is only one truth, or many truths. Similarly, it is related to ideas about creation, evolution, growth and decay. Third, the source of "being" is either transcendent or imminent. This issue is at the heart of many religious systems, in which the source of everything is identified with a god, or some other supernatural being or force. It also lies at the core of the distinction made earlier about the Platonic notion of ideal "chair-ness" and the Aristotelian emphasis on the particular concrete chair. Finally, the condition of existence is either individualistic or relational. The individualistic view has dominated the development of Western thought, particularly with respect to the sciences, finding its ultimate champion in the French philosopher and mathematician René Descartes (1596-1650), as best expressed in his famous dictum *cogito ergo sum* (I think therefore I am). The relational approach is described in greater detail in the next chapter.

John Dixon and Rhys Dogan (2002) divide ontological approaches into two categories based on alternate conceptions of where causality resides. They use the term structuralism to refer to those ontologies that emphasize external influences on human behaviour, and the term agency to refer to those theories that focus on the capacity of individuals to exercise a significant level of control over their own actions. While they observe that recent developments in social theory reflect the fact that this distinction does not match up with the way that things actually happen in the real world, they also emphasize that the development of our ideas about governance clearly reflects the influence of these two approaches. Acquiring an understanding of the relationship between structure and agency is a key component in understanding social leadership, and consequently it receives extended coverage, along with relational ontologies, in the next chapter.

The importance of understanding something about the ontological assumptions that people make regarding the world they live in can perhaps best be exemplified through an examination of what happens when a shift occurs in ontological frameworks. An excellent illustration of what amounts to a major change in the ontological underpinnings of a foundational system of thought (the U.S. legal system) can be found in the decision of the U.S. Supreme Court in the case of *Citizens United v. Federal Elections Commission*, in 2010.

In *Citizens United*, the justices decided by the narrowest of margins (5 to 4), that corporations, associations and trade unions could make independent political contributions (see Meyer 2012). The justices based their ruling on the First Amendment right of free speech. More specifically, it was based on the idea that no law should be passed that would prevent someone from expressing his or her political views on which candidate or idea to vote for or against, whether that someone was a person or a corporate body. Further, it recognized that if a corporate entity could argue for or against a particular candidate, then it had every right to independently provide that candidate with financial support. The Court's decision generated strong responses from supporters and detractors alike, and led to unprecedented amounts of money being spent by corporate interests during the 2012 elections. Focusing on the ontological shift implied in this ruling, some interesting questions arise. Are corporations, which are artificial stated-created entities, the same as natural human beings? If they are not, then on what basis should they be extended constitutional rights? If they are, then are they eligible for any and all other constitutional rights extended to citizens? Can they be charged with murder? Can they run for political office? The extent of the impact of this decision will only become clear as various parties attempt to use the decision reached in *Citizens United* as a means of justifying still-further rights-based claims founded on this ontological shift.

When talking about leadership, the almost universally accepted ontological components are leaders and followers. Furthermore, followers are most often viewed as somehow subordinate entities. In constructing ontologies, entities are often positioned within a hierarchical scheme, not just as a means to prevent confusion, but also as a way to facilitate causal explanations. By placing leaders above followers, it becomes easier within the framework of some leadership models to explain power, influence and the achievement of goals.

Knowledge and Knowing

Epistemological theories are concerned with the subject of knowing. As with other areas of philosophical inquiry, the ways in which debates have been framed regarding what constitutes knowledge and how it can be acquired have varied through the ages. Some approaches have been based on the position that knowledge is objective—external to the knowing subject. Other approaches have taken the alternate view that knowledge is subjective—internal to the knower. Most epistemological theories belong to one of the following four categories. Empiricist theories of knowledge give priority to experience and the data from our senses. Idealist epistemologies emphasize the role of intuition and the nature of the human mind. Rationalist knowledge can come not only through experience and intuition, but also through the process of abstract thought, as in the case of so-called higher mathematics or philosophy. Finally, constructivist theories of knowledge emphasize the ways in which we collectively construct our knowledge of things, rather than focusing on the objects of our knowledge.

Dixon and Dogan (2002) divide epistemological debates, with respect to governance, between naturalist and hermeneutic approaches. These two approaches correspond respectively to the empiricist and constructivist approaches just mentioned. Naturalist ways of knowing are further divided into positivist theories that reject unobservables as knowable and realist theories that accept unobservables as knowable. Hermeneutics assumes that knowledge is based on interpretations that emerge intersubjectively (between knowing subjects) as we respond collectively to the things that we encounter on a day-to-day basis. The authors state that, "hermeneutic knowledge is culturally specific and subject to severe relativism, but also dynamic and open to constant revision" (176). The word hermeneutic is derived from the name of the Greek messenger god, Hermes, who would often relay his messages in the form of riddles, leaving recipients to sort through ambiguity and misdirection in order to arrive at the intended message.

I mentioned above that my sociological approach was at least in part consistent with what is known as symbolic interactionism. Herbert Blumer (1900-1987) states the three major premises of this perspective as:

Human beings act toward things on the basis of the meaning that the things have for them.

The meaning of such things is derived from, or arises out of, the social interaction that one has with one's fellows.

These meanings are handled in and modified through an interpretive process. (1969: 2)

Clearly, Blumer's approach can be classified as a hermeneutic epistemology, with its emphasis on context and interdependence, and its focus on articulating the knowledge construction process rather than on the products that emerge.

With respect to epistemological confusion, or what might better be framed as epistemological *legerdemain*, there is no better example than an interpretative framework that emerged during the debacle over the (non-) existence of weapons of mass destruction (WMDs) in Iraq (ca. 2001). In a press briefing on February 12, 2002, at which an effort was made to explain how the U.S. Government could have made such a blunder, then-U.S. Secretary of Defense Donald Rumsfeld made the following statement:

There are known knowns; there are things we know that we know. There are known unknowns; that is to say, there are things that we know we don't know. But there are also unknown unknowns; there are things we do not know we don't know.

The reactions to Rumsfeld's epistemological proclamation varied; meeting with harsh criticism and ridicule from political opponents and the media (he received the 2003 "Foot in Mouth Award" for most nonsensical statement, from the British Plain English Campaign), but most linguists and philosophers agree that the statement was actually incredibly articulate, if not a bit deceptive.

In his statement, Rumsfeld differentiates between our processes of knowledge acquisition and the products that constitute our knowledge. Things are either known or unknown—we have acquired knowledge about them, or we have not. With respect to things themselves, some of them are accepted as known (our current knowledge base), and some of them are accepted as un-known—yet to be learned. The key with this latter category is that we know that we do not know these things. Because Rumsfeld constructs his argument around a pair of dichotomies, there must be four possible categories, but he mentions only three. Here are the four possibilities, with the first word in each pair expressing the process and second word referring to the product.

known knowns   known unknowns
unknown knowns   unknown unknowns

It is in the category of unknown knowns, missing from Rumsfeld's explanation, that the real problem emerges. How can we not know something that we know? The only way for us to do that is to ignore the facts—to deny our own ability to acquire and possess that knowledge. In essence, in an effort not only to avoid blame, but also to create an interpretation in which no blame could be attributed, Rumsfeld recast a moral and political shortcoming as an epistemological problem. Highlighting the absurdity of Rumsfeld's position and the continued use of such rhetorical tactics on the part of the U.S. Government, especially with respect to their war on terror, Slovene philosopher Slavoj Žižek observed:

> If Rumsfeld thinks that the main dangers in the confronta-tion with Iraq were the "unknown unknowns," that is, the threats from Saddam whose nature we cannot even suspect, then the Abu Ghraib scandal shows that the main dangers lie in the "unkown knowns" – the disavowed beliefs, suppo-sitions and obscene practices we pretend not to know about, even though they form the background of our public values. (2004)

Back in 1959, Peter Drucker introduced the concept of the knowledge worker and, in the intervening decades, technological advances, along with demise of manufacturing in the histori-cally industrialized nations, have given rise to a rhetoric, if not a viable economic reality, centered on what has become known as the knowledge economy—a notion introduced by Drucker in 1969 (1992). As the preceding discussion suggests, and as will be explained in greater detail in the following section and again in Chapter 5, our love affair with knowledge overshadows the need for us to recognize the far more fundamental and consequential role of our value systems.

What We Value

Axiologies answer the question of what we value. There are two essential components to an axiology, the first dealing with ethics and the second dealing with aesthetics. The subject of ethics, if not its practice, has enjoyed a rapid rise in interest over the last couple of decades, especially spurred on by events like the Enron scandal, the global financial crisis, and the Gulf of Mexico oil spill (2010), among other threats to our ideas of what constitutes right and wrong (see Blackburn 2001). The subject matter of ethics is quite complex and can be subdivided into a number of distinct areas of interest, among which concerns with morality and social justice have taken on special significance with reference to business and politics (see Gini and Marcoux 2012). Axiological ethics focuses on the idea of value, and therefore is not directly concerned with what we should do, but rather with what standard we put in place to measure our actions against.

As an example of alternate axiological ethics frameworks, the Elliott-Baily (2009) report on the cause of the 2008 financial crisis provides three different narratives, each of which relies on a fundamentally different position with respect to what we value. As a precursor to outlining the three alternatives, there are two points to take into consideration. First, to the extent that the financial crisis was a global phenomenon, there can be little doubt that it was precipitated by the meltdown of the housing market in the U.S., associated with the collapse of the sub-prime mortgage market. Second, the authors of the report recognize that the narratives we construct to explain events not only contribute to our future legislative and policy building initiatives, but also to the way that we will interpret events in the future.

The first narrative places blame for the sub-prime mortgage debacle on the social policy initiative, outlined in the *Housing and Community Development Act* of 1992 that had as its goal putting the necessary regulatory mechanisms in place so that every U.S. citizen could become a homeowner. Through the late 1990s and early 2000s, mortgage-lending institutions such as the Federal National Mortgage Association (FNMA) and the Federal Home Loan Mortgage Corporation (FHLMC), known colloquially as Fannie Mae and Freddie Mac, were required to offer an increasing number of low interest loans to individuals who, under normal circumstances, would not qualify to receive financial assistance. Those who support this interpretation of the crisis place a high value on minimum government intervention in the economy, as well as on a scaled-back regulatory environment. In other words, any efforts by a government to impose a socialist agenda—level the playing field—are contrary to its role and an impediment to the proper (natural) operation of the economy.

The second narrative suggests that the crisis was caused by the arrogance and greed of Wall Street financiers, who manipulated markets and abused investors. This narrative is nearly the polar opposite of the previous one, in that it places greater value on government regulation and oversight of financial institutions and large corporations, combined with the implementation of mechanisms for consumer protection.

Finally, a third alternative takes a distributive approach to understanding the origins of the crisis, in which an overall decline in aversion to risk on the part of all parties concerned came together to create a so-called "perfect storm." As Peter Wallison (2011: 539-40) suggests, this sort of approach really amounts to a non-explanation. It fails to explain the origins of the shift in attitude among the parties, what mechanism beyond chance contributed to these factors coming together and whether the presence or absence of any one of the factors would have led to a different outcome. While it may appear that this alternative approach constitutes obfuscation rather than an explanation, it does suggest that there are those who value security and predictability over risk and uncertainty.

The second aspect of axiology, aesthetics, is quite a different matter—and one with which people may not be so familiar—especially within the context of discussions on governance and leadership. Most commonly, the idea of aesthetics is likely to be associated with artistry, as exhibited in realms like architecture, painting, music and landscape design, but there is much more to it than that. Warren Bennis is credited with musing that leadership is like beauty—you can't define it, but you know it when you see it. This assessment is not as flippant as it may sound. Most people are likely to concede that elegant and effective leadership is a beautiful thing, but what is beauty? One common response, representative of an individualistic ontology, would be to say that beauty is in the eye of the beholder, but from a sociological perspective that sort of response just avoids the question. From a philosophical perspective, trying to determine what constitutes beauty—and related concepts like harmony and the sublime—is the subject matter of aesthetics.

Donna Ladkin (2008) outlines the elements of what it means to lead beautifully, based in part on her reflections following a performance by the musician Bobby McFerrin ("Don't Worry, Be Happy"), in which he established a complex and collaborative relationship with other performers and members of the audience. The three aspects she highlights are: (1) mastery of oneself and one's context so that you are prepared to respond in the here-and-now, in other words, expertise; (2) coherence between thoughts and deeds as well as between the content of one's message and its mode of delivery, thus authenticity, and (3) purpose, moving toward a goal that serves the common interest, thus representing an ethical dimension. In looking for philosophical roots to support her ideas, Ladkin turns to Plato and the neo-Platonist Plotinus (205-270), both of whom were concerned with discovering the nature of beauty itself rather than the nature of beautiful things. Without examining Ladkin's scheme in greater detail, what I want to point out here is that she presents a genuinely axiological approach to aesthetics, in which notions of the beautiful cannot be separated from notions of the good, thus rendering aesthetics and ethics inextricably linked.

While beauty may take center stage when it comes to aesthetics, Peter Pelzer (2002) points out that negative aesthetic notions, such as disgust, may generate the most powerful and visceral responses to things that people encounter in their daily lives. Our very aversion to considering these negative notions illustrates their power. For our purposes, acknowledging that world views have an aesthetic component means accepting that people not only have a notion of what counts as beautiful (or disgusting), but that they likely use this standard to evaluate leadership and many other social and non-social phenomena.

Hans Hansen and his collaborators (2007) suggest that the artificial and ultimately self-defeating restrictions placed on leadership research in an effort to emulate science resulted in the omission from consideration of a major component of the way in which leadership is actually practiced—gut feeling. The authors emphasize the root of aesthetics in the notion of sense perception. When we say that a certain situation smells rotten or leaves a bad taste in our mouth, it is more than mere metaphor. They demonstrate how aesthetics can be viewed as an alternate way of knowing. Just as Rumsfeld disguised an axiological issue as an epistemological one, aesthetics helps us to understand how we use our value system to determine what can be known and how we understand it.

In an article that examines the flawed leadership efforts in response to the Hurricane Katrina crisis, Ralph Bathurst et al. (2010) suggest that aesthetically aware leaders may be better equipped to manage disasters and other crises. By aesthetic awareness, the authors mean the ability to balance concern with the overarching political and economic implications of a situation with a genuine empathy and consideration for the suffering and emotional trauma of the people. As with Ladkin's analysis, the

way in which these researchers conceptualize aesthetics is inseparable from ethics.

By way of comparison, Haina Zhang et al. (2011) describe
the practice of aesthetic leadership in Chinese business, which
reflects a foundation in the ethical principles laid out in the works
of Confucius (Kong Fuzi, 551-479 BCE). Within Confucian
thought, beauty is viewed as the result of attaining harmony,
and harmony arises through self-cultivation—the integration of
individual purpose with social norms and collective wellbeing.
These aesthetic goals are realized in the practice of virtues such as
humaneness (*ren*), appropriateness (*yi*), ritual (*li*), conscientious-
ness (*zhong*) and mutuality (*shu*). Mid-level managers in eight
firms were interviewed regarding the leadership behaviours of
their superiors. Overall, the findings suggested that the practice
of aesthetic leadership is common in Chinese firms because it fits
naturally into Chinese culture. The results also showed that to
a greater extent in state-owned firms, aesthetic leadership was
adopted opportunistically when circumstances called for it, rather
than being normative. This more instrumental approach was
explained as reflecting the contrasting demands of government
regulators and the economic realities under which businesses
operate. The authors conclude that in both privately owned and
state-owned enterprises, normative aesthetic leadership which
is natural and authentic has a more positive impact on worker
motivation and firm productivity than instrumental aesthetic
leadership, which merely appropriates traditional values for strategic purposes.

Norms and Rules

Nomologies reflect our attempts to discover the laws or rules
about something. We have expectations about how things are
supposed to proceed, sometimes on the basis of norms agreed
upon within a particular social group, such as our family or community, and other times on the basis of seemingly objective sets of

rules that are viewed as existing outside of particular contexts or personal interests. Perhaps the two most common examples of the latter would be the laws of physics in the material world, and the Golden Rule in the moral realm. The subject of rules, as they may pertain to governance and leadership in organizational settings, is discussed incrementally over the next three chapters.

ooooo

In bringing this discussion of philosophical concepts to a close, the question to keep in mind as we move forward is one of the extent to which we can articulate our view of the world in terms of these four domains—ontology, epistemology, axiology and nomology. More specifically, when we think of leadership or governance, do we understand the philosophical assumptions we are making? Are they consistent with our view of what constitutes and counts in other social realms?

3. Relationships

The material in this chapter expands upon the philosophical discussion of the ontological difference between substances and relationships, first by examining relationships from a sociological perspective, and then by looking more specifically at the ways in which relational ontologies have informed ideas about leadership. The enduring influence of rationalist and individualist perspectives serve as a substantial barrier to understanding and accepting the notion that what is of greatest significance in all realms of collective social action is what is constructed in the space between participants. To close out the chapter, this sociological insight is examined in greater detail through an exploration of the relationship between agency and structure. As the material covered in this book wends its way toward a final discussion of the nature of social leadership and the embeddedness of all instances of leadership in particular governance environments, developing a robust but constructivist understanding of the interplay of agency and structure is essential.

Relational Sociology

In a 1997 article in the *American Journal of Sociology*, Mustafa Emirbayer outlines what he refers to as a manifesto for a relational sociology. His primary objective is to bring about a fundamental shift in the ontological perspective that dominates sociological inquiry: namely, one that privileges substances over relations. His use of the word manifesto in the title signals that this shift would constitute a revolutionary change, having major implications both for theory development and for the way in which empirical research is carried out. The article begins at the philosophical level drawing a distinction between a substantialist ontology, which views substances as the fundamental unit of inquiry, and a relational ontology, which gives primacy to action and process over static entities. As a means of expressing both the shortcomings and pre-eminence of the substantialist view, Emirbayer cites German sociologist Norbert Elias (1897-1990), who observed: "We speak as if a wind could exist which did not blow" (1978: 112, cited p. 283).

Borrowing his terminology from the work of John Dewey and Arthur Bentley (1949), Emirbayer divides substantialist perspectives into two types: self-action and inter-action. The self-action perspective views entities as operating, or initiating action, under their own power. There are three variations within this perspective, the first two of which are based on alternate views of the source of individual power, and the third of which focuses on structures rather than individuals. The first variation, adopted by the majority of economists, assumes the existence of rational actors, who operate independently of each other. Alternately, the second form, which was common among early sociologists as they attempted to understand the interrelated behaviour of societies, views action as interdependent, with individuals operating on the basis of internalized norms. Finally, a third alternative, also common among early sociologists, is associated with the idea that action originates not with the individual, but with larger structures, such as organizations, nations or other social systems.

The inter-action perspective is predicated on the primacy of attributes, rather than on the entities possessing those attributes. This perspective, which has come to dominate much of contemporary sociological investigation, manifests itself most evidently in variable-centred research. Action originates through causal connections among attributes, with the actual entities possessing those attributes, in a sense being abstracted out of consideration. For example, gender, race and income level, to name a few, become the driving forces of action, with the gendered individual, say, being of little or no significance. This perspective obtained, and retains, much of its academic and political appeal from the fact that it lends itself to the application of various quantitative research methods and statistical analysis. In a sort of cart-before-the-horse scenario, the allure of measurement has created a situation where the perception of epistemological certainty has taken precedence over and constrained our ontology. In other words, instead of devising ways of knowing based on the way we conceive of those entities that make up the world, the inter-action perspective leads us to reconceptualize our world view to match our ideas of how we can understand it.

The relational perspective, to which Emirbayer refers as trans-actional, focuses directly on action, without having to attribute that action to some pre-existing or static entity. Rather, in this view, things acquire their meaning, significance and identity through transaction. Thus the focus of observation and analysis shifts to the process and context, replacing the abstraction of substance in the form of variables. Similarly, point-in-time (snapshot) measurement is replaced with a focus on continuity, and an appreciation of the dynamic and fluid nature of time and space.

Emirbayer discusses the theoretical implications of the relational perspective with respect to some central concepts in sociological analysis, as well as with respect to different levels of analysis. The four concepts selected for consideration are power, equality, freedom and agency; the critical element regarding a relational perspective on these concepts is that they should not be viewed as attributes or possessions. Rather, their only real significance emerges through actions—how they are exercised. In other words, it is not the agent (leader/manager/follower) that is of consequence, but rather agency (the action taken). Citing what, at the time, was a forthcoming work (Emirbayer and Mische 1998), the author describes agency as the "engagement by actors of different structural environments [which] both reproduces and transforms those structures in interactive response to the problems posed by changing historical situations" (294). This position parallels the tenets of Blumer's symbolic interactionism and is consistent with the way in which social leadership is to be understood.

The relational perspective also calls for a reconceptualization of the standard levels of analysis (macro, meso, micro) used in sociological inquiry. The macro level of nations and societies needs to be viewed as consisting of multiple overlapping and intersecting patterns and configurations, rather than as independent and distinct geographic, historical and cultural entities. At the meso level of face-to-face encounters, it is the dynamic unfolding nature of human interaction that is important, in the vein of what Erving Goffman (1967) referred to as the "sociology of occasions." Life should be viewed as a series of what, in the realm of theater and dramatic literature, are known as French scenes. The story, or narrative, unfolds as the composition of the group of characters involved changes, through exits and entrances. At the micro level of the individual, rather than being viewed as a given, or inherent quality, the identities of human agents are constituted by recognition and naming by others, in what Alessandro Pizzorno (1991) called "circles of recognition." We are not so much who we think we are, but rather who others see us to be.

With respect to empirical research on relationships, Emirbayer discusses initiatives that are taking place in three environments, or social contexts; namely, social structure, culture and social psychology. At the time he was writing, the most developed area of relational research was with respect to social structure, especially as represented by social network analysis. Research of this type has increased substantially in the intervening period. The fundamentals of this approach, along with some important findings that will inform the idea of social leadership, will be covered in detail in Chapter 10. Regarding culture, researchers are drawing from semiotics and sociolinguistics to examine the dynamic processes of interpretation through which our symbolic systems are constructed. Examples of this approach are provided in Chapter 6. In the least developed area of research, social psychology, the relational perspective has led to explorations of the flow of emotions and the creation of interaction rituals within groups. Some elements of this approach are discussed in Chapter 4.

Emirbayer also identifies a number of perplexities, difficulties and challenges associated with adopting a relational ontology. These include boundary specification, network dynamics, causality and values. The issue of boundary specification has to do with the fact that if we accept the ongoing and ever-changing character of relations, how can we definitively demarcate a unit for study? While this problem remains highly contested, one solution is for the researcher to accept the limits of transaction as determined by the actors involved. In other words, the significance of structures, whether in the form of organizations or jurisdictions, resides not in the abstract entity, but rather in the way that people understand that structure and operate in accordance with that understanding.

Similarly, the issue of network dynamics concerns the difficulty of examining relational processes across time. This problem is particularly vexing to researchers, in that they must carry out their studies at a particular point in time—they create snapshots, not movies. These difficulties with managing space (boundaries) and time (dynamics) are related to the question of causality. As one might anticipate, within a relational framework, causality is viewed as emergent: "social actors are always embedded in space and time; they respond to specific situations (opportunities as well as constraints) rather than pursuing lines of conduct in purely solipsistic fashion" (307).

Finally, with respect to the normative elements of relational thinking, values are not seen as objective givens. Rather, as Emirbayer states: "Transactional thinking, in a word, deconstructs a taken-for-granted moral universe," replacing this with a world view which assumes that: "Values are by-products of actors' engagements with one another in ambiguous and challenging circumstances, which emerge when individuals experience a discordance between the claims of multiple normative commitments" (309).

It is easy to imagine the difficulties that many researchers find with a relational ontology as it appears to make the task of acquiring definitive knowledge—and thereby the ability to make predictions or recommendations for practice—nearly impossible. The extent of these difficulties, at least with respect to leadership, is illustrated in the next section, but do these difficulties constitute adequate grounds for rejecting this perspective? Definitely not, especially when this perspective appears to most closely represent what actually happens in the world.

Relational Leadership

More directly in the realm of leadership studies, Mary Uhl-Bien (2006) provides a survey of what are nominally referred to as relational leadership theories. What her analysis demonstrates is that some of these theories remain grounded in a substantialist (entity-based) ontology, with a much smaller number actually reflecting the shift toward a more truly relational ontology. She concludes her analysis by presenting a framework for a relational leadership theory that draws on aspects of both ontological positions. Her contention throughout is that it is more valuable to determine the benefits to an understanding of leadership that may emerge through multiple perspectives, than to spend time arguing over which perspective is best. While her conclusion about academic squabbles may have some merit, it should not be allowed to obscure a critically important point. As a first step, researchers need to be able to identify what ontological assumptions they and others are making before constructive collaboration can take place. Combining perspectives without adequate clarification of what actually constitutes those perspectives in the first place will just create an even more incomprehensible muddle than already exists.

Among the entity-based theories, Uhl-Bien includes leader-member exchange (LMX) theory (Gerstner and Day 1997), Edwin Hollander's relational theory (1978), charismatic relationships (Howell and Shamir 2005), relational self (Andersen and Chen 2002), collective self (Hogg 2001), social networks

(Balkundi and Kilduff 2005) and Joseph Rost's postindustrial leadership (1995). The common element among these alternate approaches is that they view relationships from the perspective of the individual's perception and cognition. In other words, the concept of relationship is being used here to express the position of one entity relative to another. A person is someone's boss, or spouse, or teacher.

From a relational perspective, Uhl-Bien covers relational constructionism (Abell and Simons 2000), Leonard Sayles's notion of lateral relationships (1964) and the relational leadership theories of Wilfred Drath (2001) and Kenneth Murrell (1997). As might be anticipated, the common element among these approaches is a focus on the relationship as a process of social construction that takes place in the "space between" (Bradbury and Lichtenstein 2000) individuals. In other words, these theories attribute ontological status to the relationship itself. So, it is not the fact that someone is someone else's teacher, for example. Rather, it is the fact that there is a relationship between teacher and student that cannot be reduced to the nature or perceptions of those individuals as separate and distinct entities.

The purpose for mentioning and providing citations for such a large number of alternate theories at this point is not to go into the specifics of each one, but rather to introduce the various terms and concepts that have been recruited in an effort to develop informative and useful relational theories of leadership. Clearly, researchers have identified the need to pursue this avenue of inquiry, and the variety of approaches demonstrates not only the difficulty in finding an adequate framework, but also the need to resolve fundamental issues regarding ontology as a prior step to developing an adequate theory.

Uhl-Bien goes on to develop her own relational theory of leadership that she defines as "a social influence process through which emergent coordination (i.e., evolving social order) and change (i.e., new values, attitudes, approaches, behaviours, ideologies, etc.) are constructed and produced" (668). While it is difficult to deny the role that influence plays in the leadership process, Uhl-Bien appears to be missing the mark and in some ways undermining her own efforts. Her understanding and use of influence still seems to imply that someone is influencing someone else, rather than the more genuinely relational understanding that individuals, through their efforts to communicate and understand the world around them, influence the process of meaning-construction. In the introduction to her article, she calls attention to David Hosking's (2000) notion that persons and organizations are made in, rather than makers of, processes, and yet to some extent she ends up perpetuating the very ontological confusions that she has worked so systematically to clarify and move beyond.

Starting from the premise that "language shapes consciousness and identity and therefore prefigures all forms of social relationship" (2012b: 407), Margaret Stout advocates for the adoption of a relational language of process. Stout finds inspiration for her position in the works of Mary Parker Follett (1868-1933), who was a founding figure of process-oriented administration, a perspective which focuses on the dynamic nature of organizations and human systems, recognizing that changes are not merely quantitative, but more importantly qualitative, involving alterations of substance and meaning (1924). Stout also borrows from the metaphysical writings of David Bohm (1980) and Fritjof Capra (1975, 1983), both of who brought together insights from multiple disciplinary and cultural sources to construct world views that are more holistic and inclusive than the one we have inherited from the dominant Western scientific perspective. Stout suggests that because "language creates a predisposition for particular types of social action" (410), we must develop a way of speaking about human systems that reflects insights from quantum physics, Native American spirituality, feminist paganism, pre-Socratic philosophy and Eastern mysticism. A relational language of process, therefore, is non-binary and non-discrete, as well as gerundial. By non-binary and non-discrete, she means nonhierarchical and relational. In other words, we must come to see elements like dark and light, energy and matter, female and male, not as separate, independent and contrasting discrete components of the world, but rather as existing in relation to each other, interpenetrated and inseparable one from the other. By gerundial, she means dynamic and process oriented. In a literal sense, this means adding *ing* to nouns and treating them as verbs. Beyond this it means to stop viewing the world as constituted of static entities and to start viewing the world, and everything in it, as constantly in a state of flux and flow.

In another recent article, Ann Cunliffe and Matthew Eriksen develop a notion of relational leadership "as an inherently moral and dialogical practice" (2011: 1428). They base their understanding on the concepts of ethical selfhood developed by French philosopher Paul Ricoeur (1913-2005) and dialogism from Russian philosopher and semiotician Mikhail Bakhtin (1895-1975). The essence of ethical selfhood is seeing the self as other. In this view, we all have an obligation to be responsive, responsible and accountable to others, in order to achieve a true sense of self—we must practice an ethics of reciprocity. Dialogism recognizes that conversation (social interaction) is fluid, emergent and multi-voiced. In a sense, we exist in a perpetual conversation constructed from past, present and future, and incorporating multiple changing views and judgments.

As they express it:

> leaders need to: be concerned with identifying relationships between network elements and understand relational mechanisms; think about how they use language in networked interactions; and be cognizant of the macro- and micro- processes involved in socially constructing collective activities. (2011: 1430)

Many of the ideas drawn from Ricoeur and Bakhtin point in the right direction, but there is a problem with the way in which the authors frame their conclusion.

Like Uhl-Bien, Cunliffe and Eriksen still predicate their approach to understanding leadership on the pre-existence of a person identified as the leader. In their study, the individual research subjects were senior managers, more specifically Federal Security Directors, who were facing the challenge of managing a new organizational form and function within the context of an existing array of interrelated organizations with often ambiguous, contested and well-protected domains. Neither the circumstances nor the expectations placed on them provide adequate criteria to assume that the respondents were leaders or that they were required to lead. There is no question that they needed to manage the situation, and undoubtedly some of them did it better than others. Some of them may have even displayed leadership. And, if they did, it was because it emerged out of a particular set of circumstances, in a particular situation and was generated through the interaction of a particular collection of individuals. That is the essence of relational leadership.

Agency and Structure

As stated at the outset, the approach taken throughout this book is primarily sociological, although this term will mean different things to different people. There are many distinctions among sociological theories, but they all generally address the two key issues of how social order is established and maintained, and how social change is initiated and carried out. Bringing societies together so that people can accomplish their goals and maintain a reasonable level of security and predictability in their lives is arguably a logical and humane goal. At the same time, things change—internal to our social structures and external to them. After so much effort has gone into establishing and maintaining a certain type of social order, it is often extremely difficult to alter existing systems to adapt to the changes—or drivers of change—that they are exposed to. Sustainability requires not just the stability of an established order, but also the flexibility of being able to deflect, absorb or adapt to threats to that stability. These are the issues that concern sociologists, and these issues provide the rationale for our systems of governance and the practice of leadership.

The handful of scholars that are typically considered to be pioneers of sociological thought for the most part developed their theories of society within the framework of three dichotomies: macro and micro; conflict and consensus; structure and agency. The first of these refers to the level on which social order and social change occur, at a large scale, or on a small scale. The second refers to the mechanism through which order is established or altered; do people work together through agreement, or do they have to be forced. Finally, the structure/agency distinction identifies the source of order and change. Do the actions of overriding structures determine what people will do, or do the collective actions of individuals constitute those structures?

Regarding the distinction between macro and micro, the former was usually meant to refer to analyses of society that took place at the level of the nation or state. This perspective is best represented in the works of Karl Marx (1818-1883), Emile Durkheim (1858-1917) and Max Weber (1864-1920). Conversely, micro-level analysis was directed at small groups of individuals, the family, for example. The equation of society—and hence order and change—with the state dominated much of the early theoretical development, while the micro level was viewed as less consequential, or more rightly the domain of the emerging social science of psychology, in particular, so-called social psychology. Slowly, the emphasis on the macro level lost ground, and the micro level gained in influence, especially in the work of Georg Simmel (1858-1918) and George Herbert Mead (1863-1931). As interest grew in the social significance of communities and organizations, mid-range (meso-level) theories began to be developed (see Maines 1982). Mid-range theories are now a central focus of not only sociology, but also economics and political science, as reflected in such concepts as the "glocal," sometimes used as a term for the perspective of thinking globally and acting locally, a concept with its origins, if not its exact expression, dating back almost a century to a book by Patrick Geddes (1915).

With respect to the conflict/consensus distinction, the conflict perspective is rooted in large part in the Christian notion of original sin and in the political philosophy of Thomas Hobbes (1588-1679). Hobbes thought that a strong central authority was necessary to avoid social discord and civil war. In his view, as expressed in his 1651 book *Leviathan* (2008), if left to their natural state, humans would behave uncontrollably in their own interest, to the detriment of all. The parallel Christian idea of original sin states that humans are basically born as sinful, and thus are in need of redemption. Whether that redemption comes from the Church or from civil society is a matter well beyond the scope of this book. Suffice to say that, for Hobbes, the immediate solution was to be found in citizens submitting to a social contract, whereby they handed over control of nearly every aspect of their lives to the state in order to avoid living in constant fear and destitution.

Karl Marx viewed the apparent order of society as reflecting a struggle between the interests of the bourgeoisie (rich owners) and those of the proletariat (poor workers). He thought of religion as the opiate of the masses—a means through which the powerful could keep the oppressed in a state of subjugation by promising them a better life, in the next life. His solution for altering this order, as so many failed attempts in the last century have adequately illustrated, was for the oppressed class to revolt—decisive disruption rather than incremental adjustment. Despite apparent failures at the state level, Marx's ideas still inform a number of anti-capitalist perspectives, as well as a variety of socialist and feminist theories and social movements.

Max Weber is also usually viewed as supporting a conflict approach to social order and change, but his analysis allows for a much more complex social structure and pattern of alliances than can be found in Marx's work. For example, Weber identified class, status and political affiliation (party) as key aspects of the distribution and exercise of power in society. And, as will be described in more detail in the next chapter, Weber developed the notion of bureaucracy to describe the rationalization processes that both construct and typify complex social structures, such as corporations and governments. In contrast to Marx, Weber viewed the mundane practical constraints of administration as the greatest impediment to civil liberties and human fulfillment, rather than the manipulative exercise of the more ideological weapon of religion.

Emile Durkheim took a consensus view of society. For him, order in early (primitive) societies was based on mechanical solidarity, characterized by a collective consciousness made up of shared norms, beliefs and values. In contrast to Marx, Durkheim viewed religion as the social glue for such societies, in which identity was reinforced through the performance of rituals. As modern societies developed, order was based on the division of labour and the interdependent and reciprocal nature of human relationships. We needed each other, and in order to maintain a complex society, we needed to do different things. This notion of organic solidarity would come to inform much of modern American sociological thought in the form of structural-functionalism, a framework advocated by Harvard University sociologist Talcott Parsons (1902-1979), who thought that society evolves towards a state of equilibrium through a balance of socialization and social control.

Several theorists contributed to the elaboration of structural-functionalist thought, including English philosopher and sociologist Herbert Spencer (1820-1903), who coined the expression "survival of the fittest," too often attributed to English naturalist Charles Darwin (1809-1882), the principal architect of modern evolutionary theory. Spencer thought that larger more complex societies would defeat smaller more primitive societies, a notion that would be enthusiastically adopted by big business, and which would inform various progressivist perspectives—the idea that things get better. Columbia University sociologist Robert K. Merton (1910-2003) made a significant contribution to functionalist thought through his development of the concept of deviance and the notion of manifest and latent functions. The former term refers to those functions that are intended and recognized, while the latter refers to those functions that are unintended and unrecognizable. In Merton's view, due to unintended consequences, some social structures can in fact turn out to be dysfunctional for society.

An important concept related to structural-functionalism is that of meritocracy, a term coined in a satirical essay by Michael Young in 1958. As relatively new as the term is, the concept itself is much older and is characteristic of perspectives on business and politics from many of the world's cultures. Meritocracy is the idea that power should be allocated to those who have earned it on the basis of education and experience. At a very basic level, and reflecting the way it was conceived in the thought of the ancient Greeks and Chinese, this idea is in direct contrast to notions of inheritance, generally associated with dynasties. Just exactly what constitutes merit and how it should be measured are hotly contested issues, and our educational systems have been a common arena in which these debates have been carried out. One of the key arguments against meritocracy is the so-called Peter Principle (Peter and Hull 1969), which suggests that individuals will rise through the ranks of responsibility and/or authority until they reach a level at which they are no longer competent to act in accordance with what is required of them. This idea could be interpreted as suggesting that society will work best when we all get somewhat less than we have earned—our reach should exceed our grasp.

At least among social theorists, structural-functionalist frameworks and their related concepts have been superseded by newer theoretical constructs, but they still appear to dominate much of the actual practice of organizational life, especially with respect to emphasizing specialization, control and conformity. One of the major criticisms levelled against functionalist theories is that they are unable to account for social change; indeed it is fair to speculate that much of the reason governments, corporations and communities have so much difficulty with change is because of the persistence of functionalist thought.

The distinction between agency and structure concerns the extent to which we think the individual can act upon his or her will, as opposed to primarily responding to external drivers and constraints. The ontological element of causality is central to understanding this distinction, inasmuch as those who advocate for the primacy of agency see structures as the consequence of agents in action. Those who see structure as the key element in the establishment of social order take the opposite position. The view that agency and structure are polar opposites is an extreme position, and social theorists are more likely to view these social drivers as existing along a continuum. People give up total freedom of action for the security that comes with a certain amount of structure. Just how much freedom or constraint is ideal is an open question.

As an illustration of early conceptualizations of the structure/agency dichotomy, Marx's idea of alienation and Durkheim's idea of anomie both demonstrate a dominant emphasis on the primacy of structure, while presenting very different interpretations of the exact role of structure and its consequences for agency. As an initial distinction, alienation can be thought of as something that is done to you, while anomie is something you feel. Marx used the idea of alienation to express a sort of multistage mechanism through which owners took control over the lives of workers. First, they separated workers from the products of their work, for example, by eliminating the individual craftsperson and barter, replacing them with standardized products and money-based trade. Then, they separated workers from the means of production, by collecting workers together and putting them in factories, with piecework, assembly lines and company-owned tools and materials. The next step was for workers to become separated from others—co-workers became competitors, rate-busters, or targets for jokes or bullying. Eventually, as a final step, workers became separated from themselves, as they lost their sense of identity and drive. Crushed, the masses are unlikely to even contemplate, let alone offer, any resistance. In this view, social structure destroys agency, and with it the whole foundation of what it means to be human.

Anomie is best described as normlessness—a state of not knowing the rules, of not knowing what is expected of you and where you fit in society. With anomie, a lack of structure actually creates a sort of existential anxiety (*angst*), as if unconstrained agency is too great a burden for the individual to bear. Socialization into the norms of society, and the ability to predict what tomorrow will bring and what you will be doing, provide the individual with meaningfulness and facilitate the smooth operation of society.

Another approach to conceptualizing agency and structure views them as complementary, with each aspect responding to and helping to construct the other. For example, Anthony Giddens (1984) attributed equal ontological status to structure and agency. He coined the word structuration to describe the way in which social systems like norms, rules and institutions are produced and reproduced through social interaction. For him, social structures were in a sense memories that could be called upon to facilitate everyday life.

Social constructionism, especially as developed by Peter Berger and Thomas Luckmann (1967), emphasizes the way that people establish the meanings of the things they encounter in living their everyday lives, and how—as they continue to encounter the same or similar things—these things become objectified, as if they had a meaningful and separate existence of their own. This process frees people from having to continually reinterpret many aspects of the world they live in, but it does not mean that things actually exist, outside the way in which people collectively conceive of them. Reality, therefore, is not objective (external), or subjective (internal to the individual), but intersubjective (relational).

As a final note of reiteration before moving on, the notion of relationship can cause some confusion because it represents two distinct but related ideas. First, and most apparent, it is used to describe the association of one entity to another, from the perspective of those entities. For example, a person can be someone's parent and another person can be that person's child. Second, and of increasing importance in social theory, it represents what is created in the space between entities, not from the perspective of those entities, but on its own as a product of interaction between those entities. Everyone may possess a basic understanding of parenthood, but what is of consequence for the parent and child just mentioned is their shared understanding of what parenthood means to them, and how it informs their actions.

4. Context and Structure

Capacity to Act

The goal of this chapter is to provide an initial response to questions of what governance and leadership are for, and where they take place. As stated at the outset, the answers will be expressed in terms of capacity to act. Any attempt to define leadership or governance will be left aside for the moment. At this point, there is still a need to clarify certain aspects of the conceptual framework within which these two phenomena are to be understood. So, for now, suffice it to say that the working assumption in what follows is that the goal of both leadership and governance is the creation, development and maintenance of the capacity to act of an organization; it is the organization, broadly defined, that is the setting in which these processes occur.

There is an extensive literature on the subject of capacity building, especially in the context of economic development (see Craig 2007; Kenny and Clarke 2010; Minkler 2012). Since the 1990s, the concept has formed a key component in the messaging and mission of global enterprises like the World Bank, the United Nations Development Program, and the many independent and often significantly under-funded non-governmental organizations (NGOs) that strive to help communities become sustainable. Sustainability in these circumstances is usually expressed in terms of helping communities or countries in the developing world to acquire the skills and other competencies that will allow them to accomplish their goals around economic viability and social well-being. At the same time, a number of complementary initiatives are being carried out for the purpose of organizational capacity building, through which organizations engaged in development activities undergo their own internal development process, in order to better do their work. In this regard, Allan Kaplan (2000) points out that along with developing skills and acquiring requisite material resources, organizations must also develop the seemingly less tangible assets of a conceptual framework, an organizational attitude, a vision and strategy and an appropriate organizational structure.

The notion of capacity to act, as it will be used here, is consistent with the idea of organizational capacity building and developing the sorts of assets identified by Kaplan. As such, it refers not only to establishing a storehouse of resources, whether human, material or systems related to support the activities of an organization, but also to developing the kind of shared under-standing and commitment among those involved that will allow an organization to be responsive and adaptive. Further, it is not restricted to so-called development organizations, but instead is seen as critical to the functioning of any and all organizations, irrespective of their scope, sector, structure or goals.

Context

All human activity is situational and circumstantial. Everything that happens occurs in a particular place at a particular time, as the result of some combination of precipitating factors, many of which may be difficult to identify and consequently impossible to measure. This notion may appear obvious, but it is important to stress that much of our formal (scientific) examination and analysis of human collective pursuits starts by abstracting such activity out from the time and place in which it occurs. One reason for this sort of abstraction is related to the goal of providing results that can be generalized and therefore applied to multiple settings and situations. A second reason is that you can only study what you can measure. As a consequence of both of these factors, the role and contribution of context in governance and leadership research is too often ignored or oversimplified.

Gary Johns defines context as "situational opportunities and constraints that affect the occurrence and meaning of organizational behavior as well as functional relationships between variables" (2006: 386). This definition highlights the two ways that context needs to be thought of when discussing its significance in understanding and functioning in organizations. The effect that context has in the real time unfolding of organizational life is very different from the way in which context can be retrospectively measured and analyzed in the study of organizations. Reflecting on the net effect of these two influences, Johns observes that: "Context is likely responsible for one of the most vexing problems in the field: study-to-study variation in research findings" (389).

Johns identifies seven ways through which context may manifest itself as a factor in determining organizational behaviour. While each of these aspects demonstrates independent characteristics, they very often overlap in practice. First, context may represent the salience of situational features. For example, closure of a mine or major industry in a town where this enterprise was the primary source of jobs is likely to have significant impact on the local people's views of their future prospects. Similarly, in the wake of a school shooting, we would expect to find changes not only in student academic performance but also with respect to behavioral patterns such as withdrawal or acting out. Studying, or living with, either of these events would obviously be predicated on the specifics of the situation.

Second, context can also reflect the relative strength of the situation. Strong situations can be viewed as those that are likely to constrain the expression of individual or alternate behaviours. In contrast, weak situations are those that allow for greater individual freedom of expression. Consistent with the idea of unintended consequences, however, seemingly trivial situations can often give rise to substantial changes, while ostensibly more pertinent stimuli can have little or no effect. Third, context can have a cross level affect. In other words, actions taking place at one level of an organization, or that are intended to have primary impact on one particular aspect of the organization, can affect what goes on at a different level or at a different place within the organization. Changes in accounting procedures can impact the way in which engineering or manufacturing departments do their work. Fourth, context can refer to a certain configuration or bundle of stimuli within the organization, acting together to precipitate positive or negative consequences. For example, offering training programs to employees or providing tuition reimbursements may lead to increased productivity and job satisfaction, but it may also lead to more employees leaving to take better jobs elsewhere. When these initiatives are combined with salary increases, promotions and other forms of recognition, employee retention levels may increase.

Fifth, context may reflect a singular event or action, such as a crisis like Hurricane Katrina or a change in management structure, say, from a rigid hierarchy to self-directed teams. In both cases, people's attitudes toward work, their evaluation of priorities and their patterns of behaviour in many realms of their life are likely to change. Sixth, context may have an impact as a shaper of meaning. In this respect, Johns draws attention to the so-called "frog pond effect" whereby individuals attribute meaning to events and processes based on their standing relative to others in their immediate environment rather than in absolute terms. Finally, context may be viewed as a constant. One aspect of this view is to see some component of context, such as culture, as given; in other words, it is just there. A second aspect of this view, relevant when studying organizations, is that context may be viewed as a constant—something that does not change—and consequently a factor that can be omitted from the variables taken into consideration.

In attempting to explain why context has not received the attention it deserves, Johns points to the fact that we lack a systematic and refined taxonomy within which to discuss matters of context, and that researchers studying organizational behaviour tend to focus on causal mechanisms originating with the individuals involved rather than on more macro-level variables. Because our focus is on relationships, context is especially important as a factor that can shape interaction. More specifically, context is a key component of the way in which governance structures are experienced and in which opportunities for leadership are created.

Lyman Porter and Grace McLaughlin (2006) report on the way that context is mentioned but not systematically dealt with in leadership research. Unlike Johns, who focuses on the ways in which context can influence what takes place in organizations, Porter and McLaughlin provide a list of components that constitute organizational context (2006: 562), as follows:

Culture/climate

Goals/purposes

People/composition

Processes

State/condition

Structure

Time

Of these factors, culture has unquestionably received the most attention. Terrence Deal and Allan Kennedy (2000) define organizational culture rather colloquially as "the way things get done around here." They differentiate between four types of cultures, based on three factors: the speed at which feedback is received, the way people are rewarded and the amount of personal risk involved. Work hard, play hard cultures, like restaurants and software companies, get immediate feedback and reward, and are relatively low risk. Tough-guy macho cultures, like professional sports teams and police forces, also have rapid feedback and reward, but involve substantial personal risk. Process cultures, like banks and insurance companies, have very slow feedback and reward, and are also low risk. Bet-the-company cultures, like aircraft manufacturers and oil companies, have slow feedback and reward, but are very high risk.

Edgar Schein (2010) presents an alternate view of organizational culture, looking at it from the perspective of an outside observer. He suggests that an organization's culture exists on three cognitive levels. On the surface, culture can be identified by various artifacts, such as facilities, furnishings, dress codes, frequency and style of personal interaction, and so on. This level also includes the history and myths of the organization, mission statements and slogans, as well as the language styles and vocabularies that get used and the types of rituals and ceremonies that take place, for example, to welcome and train new employees or recognize individual or corporate accomplishments. All of the items at this first level would be visible to an outsider, knowing nothing about the organization. Below this, at a level not visible to an outsider, are the values that members of the organization profess, representing their collective perspective on issues of customer service, loyalty, trustworthiness and similar matters that could be articulated in a conversation with an outsider or new recruit. The deepest level of culture is represented by an organization's tacit assumptions—the unspoken rules. These aspects cannot be readily observed or even described. Members in some sense acquire these assumptions through osmosis, over time, as they participate in organizational life and build their own identity within the organization. Schein's approach is valuable in helping us to understand the paradoxical behaviour of organizations, such as Enron (see McLean and Elkind 2003), where a particular set of values was professed and reinforced by rituals and other visible expressions, all hiding a more nefarious and deep-seated set of basic assumptions. Based on the complexity of culture and the potential mismatch that can occur between levels of culture, Schein thinks that culture is the hardest organizational attribute to change.

Climate is more an expression of the sensory impact of the environment of an organization—how it feels. So, while culture and climate are related aspects of organizational context, they are also distinct, and can sometimes be in opposition to one another.

For example, with respect to culture, an organization may have a customer service orientation, and yet, if employees are constantly being monitored and criticized for their performance, the climate might be extremely negative and stressful, undermining the over-arching culture. A negative organizational climate can also be created by so-called "toxic" employees, whose stormy personalities and manipulative practices can have a tremendous impact on the performance and stress levels of others (see Jonason, Slomski and Partyka 2012).

Culture, of course, can also refer to the influence of place on a scale beyond the organization, whether that means a local community, a region or nation. The ways in which leadership and governance are conceptualized in China are likely to be different from the ways these phenomena are viewed in Germany or the United States. Similarly, even though there might be a broadly accepted American view on these matters, it is equally likely that the perceptions of business people, politicians and academics in California, Montana, Texas and New York are going to demonstrate significant differences. At some level, there are likely to be common concerns among these Americans that could be counted as cultural, but it is equally likely that the fundamental assumptions made by people in these different locales have a significant influence on the way they perceive and understand these concepts. The matter of national and regional differences, more directly related to alternative perspectives on leadership, will be explored more thoroughly in Chapter 8.

The notion of goals and purposes can reflect a broad range of expectations regarding not only what will be produced, but also how it will be produced. These expectations can be expressed in terms of mission statements, policies and procedures, or the edicts of a particular manager. At one company I worked for, requests for technical information generated by members of the sales and marketing staff were expected to be responded to within three working days. This expectation led to a heightened sense of anxiety among the engineering and technical support staff, because they operated in a culture of providing answers with the highest possible level of accuracy and completeness. Frustrated with continual criticism from senior management about not providing adequate support to the company's key representatives, at weekly meetings, the department manager would repeat the same admonition to the technical staff—you do not need to provide *the* answer; you just need to provide *an* answer.

The idea of people and composition contains a variety of elements. First of all, it may simply imply the number of people involved. At the same time, it can refer to socio-demographic differences among individuals with respect to age, gender, ethnic background, marital status and place of residence. In small towns, people are likely to both live and work together. In large cities, employees can live at a significant distance from both work and each other. In some instances, such as the Alberta oil sands, many workers have their primary residence in regions like Cape Breton, and make the long-haul commute back home every few weeks to spend time with their families before returning to work. Another area of difference that contributes to the establishment of particular work environments is with respect to education and skill levels among employees or participants, as well as their professions and job categorizations.

The range of processes that may be taking place within any organization is likely to be a function of the type of work that the organization is engaged in. A bank will be very different from a metal processing factory. Different technologies may be in use, from deep fryers, through metal stamping machines, to various configurations of computer and communications hardware and software. Varying degrees of standardization may apply. For example, all employees may be outfitted with the same personal computer and an approved, and therefore supported, suite of word processing, spreadsheet and presentation software. Processes can also refer to a broad range of policies and procedures, as well as industry standards, such as ISO 9001 or government environmental or health regulations, under which an organization either chooses to operate or is compelled to do so.

The state or condition of an organization can refer to the condition of its current physical resources. For example, companies operating in facilities that require costly ongoing maintenance will assess their viability very differently from firms for which these matters represent a very small portion of their operating costs. Similarly, alterations in the availability of raw materials, both in terms of absolute supply and associated cost, can interfere with the ability of otherwise successful and well-run organizations to carry out their business. Financial considerations, such as cash flow, credit rating, market valuation and stock prices, are also consequential indicators of organizational health. Perhaps less obvious, but certainly no less consequential, an organization's reputation can alter its fate rapidly and sometimes irreparably (e.g., Dupont, Lululemon).

Organizations can vary with respect to size, shape and type, as well as degree of formalization and centralization. Some organizations are hierarchical, with multiple layers of management and oversight, while others tend to be flat, reflecting a broader distribution of responsibility and participation in management. The last few decades of mergers and acquisitions have led to a situation where almost every industry around the globe is controlled by a small number of super-corporations that represent complex contractual constructs which, arguably, are focused more on distribution of profits and amelioration of risk, than on the products or services being offered.

Time is a curious aspect of context. In one sense, all we have is time, and there is nothing we can do to make it pass any more quickly or slowly than it does. However, advances in communication technologies, and the explosion of social media that these advances have facilitated, have gone a long way to changing the ways in which we use and perceive time. Our drive for immediacy and our increasing felt need for instant gratification are impacting our expectations about how we work, how we measure accomplishment, what we expect in terms of rewards and how we interact with one another.

On a broader scale, though, we tend to think of time with reference to matters of scheduling and duration. Students and people working in an education environment tend to think of the year as beginning in September, and being punctuated with a series of due dates, exam periods and set vacation times. This high level of predictability with respect to workflow and other activities allows individuals to plan and prepare. The tenure of particular people in certain positions can also be a factor. For example, we are likely to find significant differences between organizations where a founder remains at the helm over an extended period and ones in which individuals in key positions are rotated through on a regular basis.

Organizations and Organizing

The heading for this section comes from the title of a book by Richard Scott and Gerald Davis (2007). It captures the fact that in some instances organizations are viewed as entities while in others they are seen as processes. Consistent with the emphasis on relationships and emergence that has been spelled out in the previous chapters, it will come as no surprise that, as we proceed, the process of organizing will be given preference over the perception of organizations as static structures. At the same time, however, we must recognize the fact that the majority perception runs counter to this. Organizations are most often viewed as structural entities reflecting order and longevity.

Scott and Davis (2007) discuss three distinct approaches to understanding organizations—as rational systems, natural systems or open systems. The rational systems approach, which has dominated research in organizational studies, views organizations as collectivities with a high degree of goal specificity and formalization. Among its earliest forms was scientific management as pioneered in the work of Frederick W. Taylor (1911), who suggested that every job could be analyzed in order to determine how to get the maximum output from the minimum input of energy and resources. A parallel development, originating in the work of Henri Fayol (discussed in more detail in Chapter 7), focused on the rationalization of administrative and management processes and procedures, again with a view toward optimization. Perhaps the most significant development, however, was Max Weber's introduction of the notion of bureaucracy and the rational-legal basis of authority that supports it.

As alluded to in the previous chapter, Weber's observations about bureaucracy were not necessarily being presented as an ideal or something to strive for, but rather as an explanation of why such systems exist, coupled with a warning about the inevitable social harm that such systems create and maintain. The two key conceptual components of a bureaucracy are sets of rules and groups of individuals who use these rules to condition human behaviour with respect to certain aspects of daily life. In Weber's view, these systems of rational-legal authority were highly impersonal and were best suited to sustain the large complex administrative structures necessary to support both the modern state and capitalism. Scott and Davis provide a concise list of the key aspects Weber identified as characteristic of bureaucratic forms (2007: 48–49).

Fixed division of labour among participants

Hierarchy of offices

Set of general rules that govern performance

Separation of personal from official property and rights

Selection of personnel on the basis of technical qualifications

Employment viewed as a career by participants

Most people will recognize these from having dealt with government agencies, schools and banks. The justification for bureaucracies, as opposed to other organizational forms, is that they provide greater stability and predictability of administrative action, while at the same time providing a solid framework within which individuals can exercise a fair level of independence and discretion in both the application of rules and resistance to the edicts or whims of their superiors (see Wilson 1988).

The natural systems approach is more process oriented, focusing on organizations as collectivities whose members are pursuing multiple, sometimes disparate, interests, and who recognize that maintaining the organization can provide a valuable resource in support of their activities. In contrast to the rational systems approach, this perspective exposes the goal complexity that exists in most organizations, as well as the importance of informal structures in accomplishing those goals. One famous illustration of this approach can be found in the famous Hawthorne studies carried out by Elton Mayo (1945) and his associates, in which the impact of group behaviour, but also the recognition of individual differences among workers, came to light. The best known finding from these studies, of course, is the so-called "Hawthorne effect," which points out that people respond as much if not more to being observed than they do to other changes, positive or negative, that are made in their environment.

In a related initiative, business executive Chester Barnard (1938) drew attention to the fact that organizations are basically cooperative systems that rely on the integration of the contributions of everyone involved. Similarly, Philip Selznick (see 1952) suggested that organizations take on a life of their own, reflecting a number of non-rational elements that emerge from individual actions and collective interactions by people who are not merely filling positions, but bringing their entire person (identity) to work.

One of the important differences between the open systems perspective and the previous two approaches is that it views organizations as part of the environment in which they exist, rather than as closed systems, somehow sealed off from the outside. This perspective accentuates both the openness to, and dependence on, the flow of information, materials and personnel that infiltrate, shape and are shaped by the organization's activities. Relationships and connectivity, as well as constant change and adaptation, are key aspects of open systems. For example, Jeffrey Pfeffer and Gerald Salancik suggest that: "The organization is a coalition of groups and interests, each attempting to obtain something from the collectivity by interacting with others, and each with its own preferences and objectives" (1978: 36). As interests change, so do alliances; creating a social setting that is loosely coupled—what in the following section will be referred to as the "Goldilocks effect."

One particularly relevant contribution to open systems theory comes from Karl Weick, who defined the notion of organizing as "the resolving of equivocality in an enacted environment by means of interlocked behaviours embedded in conditionally related process" (1969: 91). While on first reading, the abstruse language of this definition may obscure the insight it contains, it actually points to a key element of both governance and leadership. The process of organizing is one of reducing uncertainty. In order to accomplish their goals, people need to make sense of what is going on around them. Ambiguities will emerge, but enough certainty needs to be established to strike an effective balance between stability and uncertainty.

A big part of understanding organizations is related to the concept of institutions, which according to Douglass North, "provide the rules for the game, whereas organizations act as the players" (1990: 4-5). In other words, we have created various sets of rules to represent the ways we think things should be and, when we form an organization, we construct it in such a manner that it reflects our understanding and expectations. For example, we have a notion of what a bank is and what functions it should perform. So, if we decide to start a bank, we have a pattern to follow. One of the primary reasons for following the pattern is that we want people to recognize our organization as representing a certain type of institution. This quest for legitimacy leads to institutional isomorphism (DiMaggio and Powell 1983), whereby adherence and conformity have the potential to outstrip efficiency and effectiveness. This is the fate of many governance systems, in which structural integrity and the maintenance of procedural norms can divert resources away from actual accomplishment.

Leadership can also be viewed as an institution. In an effort to be recognized as leaders, individuals will often attempt to model their behaviour after that of exemplars who have been identified, publicly or in a particular context, as leaders. Ontologically, this is a curious approach, in that it would actually constitute follower-ship, rather than leadership. The circumstances and situations that gave rise to the emergence of leadership in the case of the exemplar can never and will never be reproduced. There may be lessons to be learned from what happened in these situations, but they represent the factors that contributed to the creation of an environment in which leadership could emerge—not leadership per se.

Complexity

A common sense understanding of the notion of complexity is likely to be associated with our assessment of a system contain-ing many parts, or a process requiring many steps. Interpreting complexity as magnitude or variety might be referred to as the simple way to understand the concept, in that it generally does not require, or lead to, rethinking how a system or process operates. Rather, it reflects the kind of frustration or exhaustion that arises from being presented with too many choices, or having too much to keep track of or too much to do. These "not being able to see the forest for the trees" situations can have a serious impact on performance and accomplishment but, for our purposes, we need a more complex way of viewing complexity.

As a precursor to outlining the potential impact of Complexity Theory (CT) on leadership research, Marguerite Schneider and Mark Somers (2006) describe how CT differs from General Systems Theory (GST), which has dominated organizational and leadership research for decades (Katz and Kahn 1978). The pre-dominant characteristic of all systems according to GST is that they are governed by the principle of equilibrium, or homeostasis. Systems import energy, in the form of resources, from their envi-ronment to sustain their ordered state. By contrast, CT proposes that complex systems rely not only on the consumption of external energy, but also on energy that is generated internally through the interaction of its parts, with the goal of adapting to ever-changing conditions. Schneider and Somers identify three critical building blocks of Complexity Theory: non-linear dynamics, chaos theory and adaptation and evolution.

Our understanding of non-linear dynamics developed from studies of non-equilibrium thermodynamics; that is, systems in states of extreme instability (see Auyang 1998). These systems display an emergent self-organizing quality that is more a function of the interactions of their elements than a response to external or environmental conditions. Coupled with this emergent quality is the idea of extreme sensitivity to initial conditions, otherwise known as the "butterfly effect." This metaphor can be expressed, for example, as the notion of a butterfly flapping its wings in Beijing affecting weather patterns in New York. Unlike linear systems, in which changes in a particular variable are assumed to produce measurable and proportional responses in other variables, in non-linear systems, changes in a variable—one that may not even be known or knowable—may produce disproportionately large or small responses in other variables, or even no response at all. The unpredictable nature of this phenomenon is a function of the multi-dimensional interrelatedness of the system's parts (see Anderson 1999). Of course, the other important aspect of this phenomenon is the idea that some distant and seemingly unrelated stimulus can in fact be the primary driver of some action or event. This idea of "action at a distance" led to a significant reconceptualization of our notions of space and relatedness (see Gleick 2008).

Chaos theory involves the study of the relative disorder of systems. The word relative implies that the behaviour of the system is predictable with respect to some pattern, but that neither the precise path, nor the particular temporal trajectory, can be determined (see Rosser 1999). As a starting point for grasping this curious phenomenon, it is critical to understand that chaos is not the same as randomness, in that random behaviour has no pattern. In chaotic systems, events play out within the bounds of what is referred to as a "strange attractor," a set of limiting preferences or possibilities. So, while the specific location on that attractor and when a particular event will occur cannot be predicted, a great deal can be said about what cannot happen. In the face of uncertainty, we will often say that anything is possible. Chaos theory tells that that is not the case. Only a certain, and surprisingly limited, range of things is possible—it's a question of knowing where and how to look.

Finally, complex systems have the ability to play a part in their evolution and adaptation to changes imposed from outside. Due to the interdependency of the components that make up the system, self-organization emerges as the system responds to environmental conditions. Not all systems, however, possess the same capacity to respond. Highly ordered systems like bureaucracies are too rigid, meaning that only minor changes are likely to occur, as most energy is put into maintaining the status quo. Conversely, highly complex systems such as some financial markets are too sensitive, or fragile. They expend little energy on protection or filtering, thereby running the risk of complete rupture in the face of certain external threats. Rather, it is "poised" systems (see Kauffman 1991), ones that are chaotic, in the sense of patterned but flexible, that possess the optimal capacity for evolving and adapting to changing conditions. This observation can be viewed as an example of the "Goldilocks effect" (see Turkle 2012), adapted from the story of the young girl who ate from the porridge bowls of three bears—one was too hot, one was too cold, while the third one was just right.

In Turkle's case, the effect is used to describe the fact that social media technology has allowed to us to maintain a certain level of interaction with a relatively larger number of people, than we would want to interact with on a face-to-face basis. As our social sphere expands, we want the majority of our contacts to be neither too close, nor too far away.

Communities of Practice

Communities are a form of organization that can reflect a broad range of institutional frameworks. There are communities of place that are based on identity with a specific geographic location and there are communities of interest built around a shared passion for things like quilting, the novels of Trollope or roller coasters. There are also communities of position, in which participants share a common social place, such as being a teenager, a university student or a single parent, and there are communities of circumstance made up of people sharing a common condition such as a chronic illness or being displaced from their homes. In all instances, it is commonality and a certain cohesiveness that emerges from the shared experience of that commonality that creates the community.

Academic discussions of community usually begin with reference to German sociologist Ferdinand Tönnies (1855-1936), whose distinction between a *Gemeinschaft* (community) and a *Gesellschaft* (society) not only identified how social order is established and maintained in these collectives, but how societies evolve. In his view, communities are built on a foundation of shared morals, whereas societies required more formal state legal and policy regimes. The reason for this difference is that, in community, people share norms and values and have common life experience, while societies are primarily comprised of disparate individuals with little in common except proximity. For Tönnies, this evolution was inevitable but also a step backward, in that it led to isolation and compliance on the basis of punishment.

In contrast, Durkheim viewed the evolution from mechanical and organic solidarity as positive. He suggested that, in the former social arrangement, laws were established to punish those who dared to deviate from commonly held beliefs and sentiments. In the latter form, the legal system was designed to provide means of compensation, so that all members of society could contribute to the maintenance of the organism as a whole, even when they chose to operate outside the established norms and rules. Thus, for Durkheim, the transition from mechanical to organic solidarity represented the evolution from law as repressive to law as restitutive. The maintenance of interdependence replaced the need for compliance and categorical affiliation.

Taking a somewhat different approach, Georg Simmel (1971) suggested that communities, or groups, and individuals are in a constant process of creating each other. Not only are groups made up of people, but people are also made up of groups. Part of what it means to be an individual can best be expressed in terms of the particular groups that a person belongs to. Developing your individuality means establishing your own set of affiliations. The importance of this perspective will become clearer through the exploration of social networks in Chapter 10.

Through his exploration of learning and knowledge management among people in the same craft or profession, Etienne Wenger developed the notion of communities of practice (1998). He suggests that these communities are structured around mutual engagement, joint enterprise and shared repertoire. The first of these elements involves the shared norms and collaborative relationships that bind the members together. The second aspect refers to the way in which the community is constructed and renewed through the interaction of its members. Finally, the members come to share a stock of knowledge and skills, including both literal and symbolic elements.

Wenger et al. outline seven principles for cultivating communities of practice (2002: 51):

Design for evolution

Open a dialogue between inside and outside perspectives

Invite different levels of participation

Develop both public and private community spaces

Focus on value

Combine familiarity and excitement

Create a rhythm for the community

These steps appear consistent with an open systems view of organizations, as well as with the emergent and pattern-oriented perspective of complexity theory. They emphasize relationships and they present an ontological framework that focuses more on values and actions than on entities.

5. Managing Resources

This chapter continues to explore the theme of capacity to act, with a particular emphasis on the idea that governance and leadership can be described in terms of how resources are managed. More specifically, the issue examined here is the contrast between the potential overutilization of resources for which there is little or no ownership (Hardin 1968) and the potential underutilization of resources for which there are too many owners (Heller 1998). The former concept has been studied quite extensively; in 2009, Elinor Ostrom (1939-2010) was awarded the Nobel Prize in Economics for her work on the management of common pool resources. Appreciation and application of the latter concept have been growing over the last decade, especially with respect to matters of intellectual property (see Burk and Lemley 2009). While the two concepts are generally viewed as polar opposites, within the context of trying to understand governance and leadership, it is more constructive to view them as complementary. The primary objective in what follows is to demonstrate that capacity to act is a function of the optimal use of resources.

The Tragedy of the Commons

In 1968, Garrett Hardin published an article in the prestigious academic journal *Science*, on what he viewed as a disturbing and ultimately destructive global trend, which he referred to as the tragedy of the commons. The major premise of Hardin's article is that the population problem is one for which there is no technical fix. However, what really caught people's attention was the fact that a central component of his argument was the notion that, in the absence of adequate controls, selfish individuals will exploit common pool resources to the point where those resources will be ruined for all. His ideas provoked a long stream of heated responses both positive and negative and, more than four decades later, the article remains influential in fields as diverse as ecology and economics, as evidenced by the fact that according to Google Scholar (as of late 2013) it has been cited more than 22,000 times. While it would be instructive to review all aspects of Hardin's argument, the two elements of particular importance with respect to understanding the nature of the responses generated, as well as seeing how Hardin's ideas fit with the notion of social leadership, are the identification of problems for which there is no technical solution and the concept of the overutilization of resources for which no clear ownership can be established or enforced.

Hardin's article is compact and deceptively complex. It is divided into ten sections, each of which not only provides the next step in his intricately conceived argument, but also stands alone in introducing yet another highly contested and controversial aspect of the human condition. While the article is as fresh and stimulating today as it was when it was written, understanding the continued relevance of Hardin's explanation and analysis can benefit substantially from the inclusion of some evidence and insights that have emerged in the intervening decades.

In the opening section, Hardin introduces the idea that there is a class of problems that cannot be solved by the application of conventional and dominant problem-solving techniques. Writing when he is, at the height of the nuclear arms race and Cold War, and at a time when scientific achievements and the scientific method were not only glorified, but viewed as almost limitless in their potential to solve even the most complex and enduring of the world's problems, he takes the seemingly heretical position that there are problems for which there is no technical solution.

The initial problem he draws attention to is the dilemma facing the global superpowers: that constant increases in military spending fail to result in proportional increases in national security. This is a rather prescient observation given the situation we are facing today, where, according to the *Stockholm International Peace Research Institute Yearbook 2013*, U.S. military spending is at a level of $682 billion per year, representing thirty-nine percent of the global total. Even though this number represents a decline since 2011, it is 50 percent higher than the level at the time of the September 11, 2001, bombing of the World Trade Center. Has this increased spending, along with the establishment of the Department of Homeland Security in 2002, and the passing in 2001 with extensions in 2006 and 2011 of the *Patriot Act*, done anything to lower the threat of terrorism in the last decade? Are there fewer wars? Recent essays by Cindy Williams (2013) and Melvyn Leffler (2013) suggest that serious cuts to military spending in the U.S. could actually provide greater security, through efficiencies and better planning, but surely there is more to it than that.

There is no arguing with the fact that scientific and technical advances in the past four decades have been spectacular, especially in the realm of information systems and communications, not to mention medical diagnostics and materials science. However, whatever benefits to society these advances have produced, in many instances, they have given rise to a whole new set of problems, many of which do not lend themselves to a type of technical fix consistent with the technology that produced them; for example, cyber-bullying.

Sunny Auyang states that:

Technology is an umbrella term that includes not only the ability to manipulate things but also the skills to organize humans and channel capital; not only the knowledge of science, engineering, management, and finance, but also the application of the knowledge in concrete situations. Knowledge accumulates, but the application of the knowledge in concrete situations may not always increase productivity. The real world is much more complicated than the idealization of the sciences, so that applications are always made with incomplete knowledge. (1998: 284)

Among the issues raised by Auyang are the fact that our use of the word technology actually encompasses a much broader range of knowledge categories than we generally associate with the term, and the idea that knowledge of any kind is always partial. Further, it draws attention to the fact that technology must be applied to concrete situations and is therefore contextual. What works in one instance may not work in another. There is no objective or detached technology, out there. Just what constitutes technology at any given moment is dependent on the situation and circumstances under which it is applied.

Like technology, leadership can be viewed as an umbrella term. There is no way to make a definitive statement about what counts as knowledge about leadership and how it should be applied. Our knowledge of any situation is always incomplete, and our application of knowledge is always fragmented and far less rational and systematic than we would generally like to imagine. From a philosophical perspective, what this implies is that the analysis of leadership, whether academically, or at a more public level, has focused too much on epistemological matters and not enough on ontological and axiological concerns. Leadership is something for which there is no technical fix.

The second issue that Hardin introduces is what he considers to be the most important problem facing society; namely, the population problem. He suggests that the dilemma we face is one of dealing with the negative effects of overpopulation (e.g., hunger, disease, unemployment) without relinquishing any of the privileges we currently enjoy—the primary example of which is the freedom to breed. As yet another reminder of the context in which Hardin was writing, it is instructive to remember that the world's population in 1968 was barely half of what it is today. Since then, life expectancy has increased by at least a decade for people living in developed countries and by more than double that in some developing countries.

In the face of world hunger, as one consequence linked to population increase, scientists have developed new varieties of grains and other foodstuffs that produce higher yields, grow effectively in harsher climates and are resistant to insects, fungus and other pests. While selective breeding has played an important role in the development of these varieties, genetic material from unrelated species is increasingly being blended to create so-called transgenic organisms. The global leader in this initiative is Monsanto (Glover 2010), and the seeds from these genetically modified varieties require specially designed pesticides, herbicides and fertilizers, all produced by Monsanto, in order to provide the crop yields and nutritional value they were designed to deliver. Some would argue that rather than addressing the issue of world hunger, Monsanto has turned agriculture into a global economic enterprise founded on the near monopolistic control of intellectual property and the complete supply chain of agricultural inputs (Robin 2010). This example amply illustrates what Hardin points out as the fallacy undermining our faith in technical fixes—the assumption that problems can be solved in the absence of any substantial change to human values or morality.

Hardin goes on to take a closer look at the population problem, starting with the observation by Thomas Malthus (1766-1834) that human population tends to grow exponentially (1798). As a result, an individual's share of the world's resources decreases significantly as population increases, assuming that the world we live in is finite. Certainly, our experience with global climate change, irrespective of whether we think it is a natural phenomenon or a consequence of human activity, should have us convinced not only of the finiteness of our planet, but also of the interrelatedness of all components of the global ecosystem.

In the 1960s, in an atmosphere of optimism, fantasy and liberation, perfectly captured in then-popular television programs like *Lost in Space* (debuted 1965) and *Star Trek* (debuted 1966), the finiteness of our planet was treated as an opportunity and a motivation for scientific and technological advancement. Hardin categorically dismisses these visions, stating rather tersely that:

"Space is no escape" (1968: 123). This is an intriguing remark, given that the U.S. was about seven months away from landing a man on the Moon (July 20, 1969). The level of scientific and technological achievement associated with the Apollo missions, and the space program more generally, was perhaps the most prolific and comprehensive since the Second World War. It is interesting to speculate, however, the extent to which the achievements, as was the case during the war, reflected a moral imperative, in that instance to prevent the establishment of a new global power, whether German or Japanese, and, in the case of the Moon landing, as a memorial to John F. Kennedy, but also as a piece of anti-Soviet bluster. Looking at the matter in philosophical terms, with respect to the causal aspect of ontology, we observe that the historical record appears to suggest that axiology drives epistemology. In other words, our values drive our knowledge production—a lesson certainly made clear by Donald Rumsfeld in regards to WMDs. Given this causal relationship, values are clearly an integral part of those entities that constitute our world view. In other words, values are not solely an axiological concern, but are also a key aspect of ontology.

Hardin points out that a finite world can only support a finite population and so there must come a time when the rate of population growth equals zero. The issue then becomes one of whether it is possible, as per Jeremy Bentham (1748-1832), to provide the greatest good for the greatest number. Unfortunately, Bentham's goal is unattainable for two reasons. First, it is mathematically impossible to maximize for two variables at once—if population goes up quality of life must go down and vice-versa. Second, it is biologically impossible because of the energy demands, primarily in the form of calories from food, required to maintain the population, let alone provide energy for work or enjoyment. Hardin argues that in order to provide for the discretionary use of resources the optimum population must be much less than the maximum that the planet can sustain. The difficulty, of course, lies in determining what number constitutes the optimum. And, further, on what basis are we going to decide what sacrifices in terms of quality of life we are willing to make to allow people to continue to reproduce?

Hardin suggests that no progress will be made in this regard until we abandon the laissez-faire approach to reproduction. In his *The Wealth of Nations* ([1776] 1964), Adam Smith (1723-1790) introduced the idea of the "invisible hand," which claims that rational individuals acting in their own best interest will in fact contribute to the greater social good. It is this notion that informs free market capitalism and leads to such economic policy positions as advocating for low tax rates for the richest members of society, because what we might view as their self-serving greed actually serves as the primary mechanism for job creation (see Boushey 2012). When it comes to reproduction, Hardin questions whether individuals can be trusted to control their fecundity so as to produce an optimum population.

The discussion then shifts to the topic that would not only become the title of the article, but which would attract the most critical attention—the tragedy of the commons. Hardin borrowed the notion, if not the exact expression, of a tragedy of freedom in the commons from a pamphlet written against Adam Smith's ideas, by an amateur mathematician named William Forster Lloyd (1833). Tragedy, as used by Hardin, is not to be equated with the idea of unhappiness, but more philosophically, in the words of Whitehead, as residing "in the solemnity of the remorseless working of things" (1948: 17). We appear to be trapped in a certain way of behaving, and that is the tragedy.

The example that Hardin uses to explain the concept is that of a shared pasture, where individual herdsmen attempt to raise as many cattle as they can, benefitting from the proceeds generated by the additional animals, while incurring only a fractional cost associated with the inevitable overgrazing of the pasture. The tragedy emerges as each herdsman is compelled, economically, to increase his herd size, without limit. As Hardin states it:

> Ruin is the destination toward which all men rush, each
> pursuing his own best interest in a society that believes in

the freedom of the commons. Freedom in a commons brings
ruin to all. (1968: 1244)

As critics would point out (see Heller 2013), one of the major
problems with Hardin's argument is that he fails to differentiate between an open access commons, in which no one can be
excluded, and a group access commons, where the number of
potential users is limited by some factor, such as geography. We
will return to this issue later in the chapter, when discussing the
optimal use of resources.

As a means of demonstrating that taking resources out of a
commons is not the only way to bring about ruin, Hardin draws
attention to the environmental impact of pollution. Whether it is
sewage, chemical run-off from manufacturing processes, smoke
stack emissions, or any one of countless other ways in which
human activity not only consumes resources, but produces some
form of waste, making resources unusable is just as tragic as
overusing them. As with overuse, the individual cost associated
with polluting is fractional and distributed among the global
population, while the benefits accrue directly to the individual.
Everyone is harmed incrementally by the exhaust fumes coming
from your car, and from your part in contributing to congestion
on the roadways, while you alone gain fully from the freedom
and convenience that driving provides. At the same time, both
mechanisms are population problems, in that an increased number of users or polluters pushes us further along the path to our
own destruction.

Shifting his attention to the ethical side of the problem,
Hardin cites Joseph Fletcher's observation (1966) that, "the
morality of an act is a function of the state of the system at the
time it is performed" (1968: 1245). The point he is trying to
make in citing Fletcher is that context and circumstance matter
when it comes to judging the morality of human activity. Old
systems of morality that deal in absolutes are unable to deal with
our current reality, characterized by excessive population and
conflicting interests. Despite its rigidity, statutory law, with its
emphasis on prohibition, has not been abandoned, but it has

been augmented by administrative law (laws which regulate the activities of government agencies), as a means of introducing and managing discretion and the evaluation of circumstances in the way we assess the permissibility of certain human actions. As a caution, however, Hardin cites the first-century Roman poet Juvenal—*Quis custodiet ipsos custodes?*—who watches the watchers? Temperance, operating with the right balance of freedom and control, means the establishment of bureaucracies, but feedback mechanisms are needed to ensure honesty and fairness.

Building on his assessment of the contextual basis of morality, Hardin returns to the population problem with the proclamation that freedom to breed is intolerable. In a world where the laws of nature prevailed, overbreeding would take care of itself, because parents would not be able to care for an increased number of children, if they had to rely on their resources to do so. Hardin points out, however, that we have chosen to create an overarching welfare state, in which care for children becomes a collective responsibility. Freedom to breed becomes integrated with the notion of equal rights for all, as codified in the following United Nations proclamation:

> The Universal Declaration of Human Rights describes the family as the natural and fundamental unit of society. It follows that any choice and decision with regard to the size of the family must irrevocably rest with the family itself, and cannot be made by anyone else. (1968: 1245)

In Hardin's view, this liberal position is categorically invalid and socially irresponsible, ultimately driving us all the more quickly toward the inevitable tragedy that we appear helpless to prevent.

Reflecting a rather grim and pessimistic view of humanity, Hardin goes on to suggest that we would be foolish to believe that breeding could be controlled through an appeal to conscience. Rather, he suggests that conscience, whether genetic or what might now be called memetic (see Dawkins 1976), is self-eliminating, as those who choose not to breed will become an increasingly lower percentage of the population, leaving the world inhabited by those who reproduce the most.

Further, he suggests that the appeal to conscience leaves us in a double bind. If people do not control their reproductive habits, then they are open to condemnation as irresponsible citizens. If they do produce fewer children, then they are likely to be condemned as simpletons, while others take advantage of the opportunity. This sort of "damned if you do and damned if you don't" conundrum leaves people vulnerable to being manipulated through guilt, to serve the ends of repressive governments, organized religion and formal education systems. Hardin observes that no good has ever come from feeling guilty, and that, in a more positive light, appeals to conscience are being crafted as appeals to responsibility. However, as he states it: "Responsibility is a verbal counterfeit for a substantial *quid pro quo*. It is an attempt to get something for nothing" (1968: 1247). Rather, he argues that genuine responsibility is a product of definite social arrangements.

The social arrangements that Hardin has in mind are ones that create coercion, but it must be mutual coercion, mutually agreed upon. In other words, a majority of people must accept the fact that certain constraints are going to be put in place and tolerated as beneficial to all. Like taxes, people do not need to like these social arrangements, and it is likely that such systems will not be perfectly just. The alternative to such an approach is the elimination of the commons through the extension of the private property regime to all aspects of life. Whichever path is chosen, Hardin is adamant that we cannot do nothing. In fact, retaining the status quo by operating as we always have disguises its own evils, particularly, as will become clear in Chapter 11, in the form of entropy—the relentless loss of order and capacity that results from failing to put adequate energy into a system.

By way of conclusion, Hardin introduces what some might view as the paradoxical position that people have the most freedom within a mutually agreed upon system of constraints (laws). This notion is succinctly summed up in a line Hardin borrows from the German philosopher Hegel (1770-1831), that: "Freedom is the recognition of necessity" (1968: 1248). For Hardin, the key necessity that needs to be recognized and acted upon is the necessity of abandoning the commons in breeding. From his perspective, controlled population growth means freedom to pursue loftier goals.

Xavier Basurto and Elinor Ostrom (2009) suggest that one of the major problems with Hardin's analysis is that he presented his notion of the tragedy as a universal phenomenon. Alternately, they explain that:

> Overharvesting frequently occurs when resource users are totally anonymous, do not have a foundation of trust and reciprocity, cannot communicate, and have no established rules. (2009: 255)

They draw attention to several examples, including inshore fisheries, forests, irrigation systems and pasture, where users have developed norms and more formal rules to manage the resource and prevent tragedy. Looking at the problem more broadly, they caution that, in order to move beyond the tragedy, we need to avoid falling into two analytical and policy traps. First, we need to beware of developing and instituting panaceas—"one size fits all" solutions. Second, individual parties need to stop asserting that their case is unique, and therefore not subject to existing or emergent normative or regulatory frameworks.

The Tragedy of the Anticommons

In an 1838 (1963) book where he introduced mathematical rigor to the study of economics, Augustin Cournot (1801-1877) described the phenomenon of a complementary oligopoly (Kosnik 2010). He explained this concept using the example of the manufacture of brass, which requires both copper and zinc. If the suppliers of copper and zinc are independent firms, then it is in their economic best interest to hold up production of brass by demanding monopolistic rents for their input commodity. The resulting high price and limited supply of brass would ultimately lead to both market inefficiency and social harm.

Expressing a similar notion to Cournot, and placing it more directly in the context of Hardin's insights, Michael Heller (1998) coined the term anticommons, to describe those situations where over-regulation, often represented by multiple ownership, could lead to the underutilization of a resource. Heller's initial insight was based on a peculiar phenomenon that emerged in Russia as economic reforms were introduced. The existence of multiple property rights holders meant that no agreement could be reached on how retail property should be managed, so storefronts remained empty, while vendors set up kiosks on the street to sell their goods.

Within the realm of intellectual property, Heller and Rebecca Eisenberg (1998) examined the potential of patents to inhibit biomedical research, particularly with respect to the development of potentially beneficial drugs for the treatment of Alzheimer's disease and various cancers—illnesses that generate significant economic and social costs. A more extensive exploration of biotechnology patents by Dan Burk and Mark Lemley (2009) demonstrated that while there is no conclusive evidence that an anticommons exists with respect to research and innovation, problems are likely to occur when trying to bring new products to the market. Similar issues have been uncovered with respect to the development of new technologies (Ziedonis 2004) and regarding copyright (Parisi and Depoorter 2003; Campbell 2010). Heller explores the broader implications of the anticommons phenomenon, in his aptly titled 2008 book, *Gridlock Economy*.

Lea Kosnik (2012) examines the anticommons in river-basin water usage in the United States. She identifies nineteen federal regulatory agencies and, within each state, up to twenty-four local agencies all claiming jurisdiction over some aspect of river-basin water use. More specifically, she discusses the way in which these multiple rights holders impede the development of small-scale hydroelectric projects that could supplement local energy needs.

By way of possible solutions, Kosnik offers three approaches. First, she suggests structural reform, whereby none of the existing agencies would be eliminated or forced to alter their regulations.

Instead, a lead agency would be identified to coordinate the processes involved. Kosnik rightly recognizes that this fix would add yet another layer of bureaucracy to an already overly complex system. Second, she suggests organizational reform, in which some of the relevant agencies would be eliminated, thereby reducing duplication and fragmentation. The implementation of this alternative would likely be highly political, as it is difficult to imagine that any organization would voluntarily want to give up some aspect of its jurisdictional claim. An instructive First Nations example of this process can be found in the efforts of Mi'kmaw organizations to sort out the regulatory environment with respect to moose hunting and fishing (see Huber 2009). Finally, she offers the less drastic third alternative of modest reform, which she divides into four categories: guidelines, information, standards and opt-in default.

Guidelines would provide a sort of map to help applicants navigate their way as efficiently and effectively as possible through the various steps required for project approval. By information, Kosnik is referring to a range of elements including electronic forms, help by phone or email, as well as document distribution and sharing between agencies. The idea of standards refers to standardization of information required, format of documents, and other factors that would alleviate the need for applicants to basically re-learn the process at each step. The opt-in default would be a major change from the current practice of opt-out. Now, an agency has a certain time period (e.g., 30 days) to opt-out of an application process, meaning that applicants have to wait to see if they will have to deal with one agency or another, before they proceed. If the default was changed to opt-in, then applicants could progress with their applications on the basis that all relevant agencies wanted to have their say. If an agency then decided to opt-out the applicant would not be delayed.

The problem that Kosnik identifies is very real and likely results in massive underutilization of resources, not to mention extreme frustration among those who want access to those resources, for whatever purpose. However, her proposed solutions clearly illustrate just how futile and ineffective it is to attempt a technical fix. It is a sad statement about the moral fabric of humanity that we are too often stuck dealing with the symptoms and not the disease.

In a study that examines the symmetry between commons and anticommons dilemmas, Sven Vanneste et al. (2006) discover that anticommons situations generate greater opportunistic behaviour than commons situations. In other words, it appears that individuals are more likely to act in ways that tend toward underutilization than they are to act in ways that tend toward overutilization. This finding can be restated as illustrating the predominance of concern with structure over agency, and the paradoxical situation that structure is what we rebel against most.

Marena Brinkhurst introduces the notion of the shadow of the anticommons to describe "a situation where a gridlock of those formally in control of resource management encourages uncontrolled informal resource use, potentially developing into situations of open-access resource depletion" (2010: 140). She examines the struggle to control India's 63 million hectares of wasteland, of which some 40 million hectares are considered available for use. On the macro scale, various levels of government and industrial concerns in the country want to see the land used for producing biofuel crops. On the micro scale, poor villagers use the land for grazing animals, collecting firewood and growing small amounts of food—an estimated $5 billion U.S. contribution to the income of these families. Brinkhurst identifies nineteen different stakeholders representing central, state and local governments, and various agencies (e.g., agriculture, forestry, rural development) within these governments, as well as local councils of elders, religious leaders and local users. The complexity of the relationships among these rights holders leads to a situation where genuine control of the resource is practically impossible to establish. The shadow effect that she points to is the paradoxical increase in exploitation that results from uncoordinated and uncooperative efforts to restrict the use of a resource.

Optimal Use

Recently, Heller (2013) has attempted to clear up some of the confusion that exists in understanding both forms of tragedy, while at the same time offering a way forward in terms of an alternate conceptualization of the relationship between ownership and the optimal use of resources. A large part of his analysis involves pointing out that our understanding of these tragedies has been hampered by the tendency of researchers to express the central issues in terms of dichotomies. So, for example, Hardin's original formulation positioned the commons as the polar opposite of private property. Heller's introduction of the anticommons altered this arrangement, such that private property is more properly understood as a middle position between the two extremes. The validity of this perspective was established by economists James Buchanan and Yong Yoon (2000), who demonstrated that the highest total value from a resource emerges when a single decision maker controls it.

Heller goes on to explain that another conceptual trap developed out of Hardin's failure to distinguish between an open access commons, where no one can be excluded—the tuna fishery provides an interesting example—and a group access commons, in which a limited number of commoners can exclude outsiders. Parallel structures exist in the anticommons realm, where the extreme case of full exclusion is offset by the notion of group exclusion, in which multiple owners or stakeholders can block each other from engaging in excessive and ultimately collectively destructive behaviours.

What emerges from the correction of these dichotomies is a spectrum of ownership, representing five separate arrangements: open access commons, group access commons, private property, group exclusion anticommons and full exclusion anticommons. Heller suggests that the existence of a genuine open access commons or a full exclusion anticommons is likely to be rare, and that the other three possibilities all allow for management through market-based, cooperative and regulatory solutions. The precise approach to management will reflect the particular situation and circumstances, but the goal remains the same—balancing ownership and use. As he states it:

> Much of the modern economy—corporations, partnerships, trusts, condominiums, even marriages—can be understood as legally structured group property forms for resolving access and exclusion dilemmas. We live or die depending on how we manage group ownership. (2013: 18)

Consistent with the observation made by Basurto and Ostrom that some resources are very well managed by groups of users, Carol Rose (1986) introduces the notion of the "comedy of the commons," by which she means that as people work together to resolve commercial issues related to common property, the collective action can have positive social benefit. Rose is in no way trying to suggest that resolving collective action problems is a laughing matter. Rather, she derives her notion from the colloquial expression, "the more the merrier," which, among other things, speaks to our fundamental need for belonging and participation. The First Nations example of five Mi'kmaw bands working together to preserve the ancient burial ground and coastline at Malagawatch illustrates this phenomenon (http://www.uinr.ca/2011/01/work-underway-to-protect-malagawatch-cemetery/). In the context of governance and social leadership, resource management regimes are systems of governance and, if we want to maximize the potential for leadership to emerge, then these systems must be designed in such a way that they lend themselves more to comedy than tragedy.

6. Meetings

Whenever the subject of meetings is raised, you can expect to be greeted with a good deal of eye rolling, heavy sighs and a plethora of horror stories. Among the opinions expressed will be the common assessments that most meetings are a waste of time, most meetings are poorly run and most meetings accomplish very little if anything at all. No matter what the context, and irrespective of the specific contributing factors, it is fair to suggest that most people do not like meetings. In fact, there is a well-known aphorism that, if you find someone who does like meetings do not put them in charge of anything. At the same time, however, there is a sense in which all occurrences of social interaction can be considered as meetings. Consequently, we might expect that scholars from a range of disciplines interested in studying human collective behaviour would have subjected meetings of various kinds to extensive and systematic exploration. And yet, this does not appear to be the case. Given the frequency and variety of meetings, the relatively small amount of scholarly attention they have received raises the issue of what we would hope to learn by studying them. Among the sorts of questions we would like answers to are what they are for, how they are constituted and carried out and why, despite their ubiquity and pervasiveness, they are viewed so negatively.

Getting Together

In one of the first book-length academic explorations of meetings, anthropologist Helen Schwartzman defines them as:

> a gathering of three or more people who agree to assemble for a purpose ostensibly related to the functioning of an organization or group, for example, to exchange ideas or opinions, to develop policy and procedures, to solve a problem, to make a decision, to formulate recommendations, and the like ... characterized by multiparty talk that is episodic in nature. (1989: 61)

At the risk of oversimplification, this definition suggests that if three or more people get together with a purpose in mind and they take turns talking then it's a meeting. Sounds simple enough. However, the use of the word ostensibly seems to imply that meetings may in fact be called merely for the sake of meeting, without any of the participants, including the person convening the meeting, having any notion of what is expected of them, or how the meeting will contribute to the functioning of the organization. Similarly, it might imply that the talking that takes place may or may not have anything to do with the purpose of the meeting. Following the example of our analysis of Rumsfeld's famous known unknowns fiasco, a two-by-two matrix can be constructed to demonstrate how these elements can be combined to create a particular kind of meeting.

Based on Schwartman's definition, meetings and talk can either be purposive or for their own sake, as pictured here:

	purposive	for its own sake
meeting	A	B
talk	C	D

I have arbitrarily labeled the four possible combinations as A, B, C and D. Some people might assume that if there is a meeting, there will be talking, and that is certainly what Schwartzman is suggesting. Similarly, as I have suggested, if there is talking, then there is a meeting. Accepting these two assumptions then the possible scenarios are AC, AD, BC and BD. From a strictly instrumental standpoint, the ideal meeting is AC, where both the reason for gathering and the discussion that takes place are centered on contributing to the operation and goal attainment of the organization. However, even when the reason for meeting is legitimate, the discussion may not focus on relevant issues (AD). When a meeting is called for its own sake (e.g., because it's Tuesday afternoon, and we always meet on Tuesday afternoon) and the talk consists primarily of idle chatter or the senseless repetition of things already known (BD), then time is being wasted and participants may become frustrated or apathetic. Rare perhaps is the situation where a meeting is called for its own sake (BC), but as a happy accident some pertinent discussion takes place and some contribution to organizational wellbeing results. The problem with this latter case, of course, is that it cannot be planned for or counted upon. Even though scenario AC may be held up as the ideal to be attained in all cases, all four combinations occur in the real world of lived human experience, and all of them contribute to the construction of who we are, what we do and how we evaluate the way time is spent.

Schwartzman's ethnographic study of meetings at an American mental health center led her to observe that meetings are integral to the processes of sense making and validation, and that "they generate the *appearance* that reason and logical processes are guiding discussions and decisions" (1989: 42). The author's exposure of this widespread and generally accepted epistemological subterfuge, which some may interpret as a rather damning condemnation of the whole enterprise of gathering to talk, actually serves to highlight the critical importance of meetings in establishing and maintaining social order. This latter point is emphasized in Schwartman's closing remarks, when she states that, "it is in meetings that we come to know ourselves and our social systems" (1989: 314).

From a mechanical perspective, meetings can differ with respect to size, duration, location, purpose and degree of formality. The multiple ways in which these variables can be combined means that our experience of participating in meetings will differ significantly from situation to situation. At the same time, the social dynamics of the meeting process are similar in all cases. Participants either talk or they listen. They may be doing a lot of other things besides that which will contribute to what messages get communicated, but for now we will privilege verbal communication as the primary activity that people engage in, in constructing the actual content of a meeting.

With respect to size, a conversation between two people or addressing a gathering of thousands will have very different rules of interaction. Similarly, a thirty second chat with a coworker at the coffee machine will have a very different feel from a two day plenary session of a large national or international association. As these two observations suggest, I differ with Schwartzman in that I include meetings that take place between only two people, such as job interviews, performance reviews and the many one-on-one chats that occur over private (personal) matters, or business-related matters to be kept from others. I also think it is important to consider meetings with a large number of attendees, because the necessarily limited opportunities for participation will mean that a significant percentage of individuals will play only a passive role during the actual meeting. What they do in smaller groups outside the meeting is a separate, but actually quite significant, issue. The subject of duration and the related issue of frequency will be discussed in more detail in the final section of the chapter.

With respect to location, Birte Asmuss and Jan Svennevig (2009) draw attention to what they call the situational characteristics of a meeting. Among these is the actual meeting room, which in an architectural sense can differ in size and shape, floor covering, wall finish, lighting, number and location of doors, climate control and whether there are windows or not. Within the room, differences can occur regarding the size and shape of the table, the seating arrangement and the type of chairs, the existence of whiteboards, screens, projectors, and whether there are pens and paper, pitchers of ice water, glasses and little bowls of candies. The authors suggest that these physical elements can all have a positive or negative influence on what exactly takes place in a meeting. Cultural norms, such as the preference among First Nations groups for "talking circles" (see Wilbur et al. 2001), can also be a factor. And, of course, participants will respond differently to these elements based on their personal preferences.

Another important factor related to location is whether a meeting takes place inside or outside of an individual or group's regular work environment. Meeting on home turf can give some participants a distinct advantage over others who may be unfamiliar with the surroundings. In all of these cases, there are only a few purposes for coming together. In a meeting, you can inform, direct, deliberate, decide or provide fellowship.

Starting with the last activity on the list, eliminating opportunities for fellowship at meetings has become a popular austerity measure among many organizations and associations. This move has taken the form of cutting back on coffee and snacks, and trimming gathering time before meetings, as well as break times during meetings. Adopting the stance that meetings are for carrying out business—if people want to socialize they can do so on their own time—demonstrates a total lack of understanding of human nature, and runs contrary to the bulk of experience that people have in almost every aspect of their lives. Strengthening bonds and establishing a shared sense of experience are key benefits that derive from all meetings, and it's fair to suggest that the bulk of what constitutes these benefits emerges to a greater extent at the coffee table than at the meeting table. As an interesting parallel, research has found that shared family meals benefit the health and wellbeing of children, through supporting language development, improving academic performance, and reducing the risk of eating disorders and substance abuse (Fiese and Schwartz 2008).

Returning to those activities that some might consider to be more directly associated with the substance of meetings, providing information can range from a single word response to the proverbial, "How was your day?" to a more formal prescribed report delivered on a regular basis outlining pertinent activities carried out by an individual, a committee or team since the previous meeting. In some instances, items are presented for information only, implying that they are not open for discussion at the meeting, or that their content is outside the jurisdiction of the group receiving the information. Announcing your recent engagement to your significant other, your imminent departure from the organization or some administrative edict (e.g., all expense claims must submitted by Tuesday at noon in order to be payable on Friday) will all contribute to the shared store of knowledge that constitutes the meaning system under which members of the organization operate. The relative importance of any piece of information, however, is not an inherent property of that information, but rather a function of when and how that information might be used.

Bringing people together to provide direction is a common supervisory task. In some settings, such as construction projects, the daily weather conditions and the availability of human and material resources can mean that the tasks to be performed that day can only be determined immediately prior to the start of work.

The acts of informing and directing can often be one sided, requiring little if any feedback. Therefore, we might expect that meetings where these are the primary objectives would be of relatively short duration. However, meetings in which deliberation and decision-making take place are likely to consume more time and require a more formalized structure, as well as a good deal more preparation on the part of participants. The substance of these latter meeting forms is primarily talk, and in order for talk to be constructive it relies on the establishment and maintenance of conversational norms—what might be considered rules of engagement.

Talk

Just as Schwartzman pioneered the systematic study of meetings, Deirdre Boden (1994) was among the first scholars to view business as talk. In particular, she used conversation analysis (Sacks et al.

1974) to explore in fine detail the way that language use produces structure in meetings and in organizational life more generally. Her conclusion is similar to Schwartzman's, stating that meetings are "*the* interaction order of management, the occasioned expression of management-in-action, that very social action through which institutions produce and reproduce themselves" (1994: 81).

The use of conversation analysis and its related approach, discourse analysis (Harris 1952), has dominated the research output with respect to meetings. The core of these methods is the way in which they examine the elements of language, including inflection, pacing, pauses, tone, volume, word selection, phrasing and what might be considered non-word use, such as grunts, sighs, coughs and laughter. Researchers have developed an elaborate toolkit for coding and interpreting what takes place in conversation, and their findings illustrate much of the inexact and contingent nature of social interaction. They also demonstrate that the mundane and seemingly unsophisticated actions and behaviours of everyday life can have as much if not more impact on the way that organizations are structured and operate than do efforts to implement loftier notions of vision, mission and mandate.

For example, in a study of women chairing meetings in two agricultural co-operatives in rural Zanzibar, Irmi Hanak (1998) examined the ways in which realizations of politeness and powerless speech style can balance out asymmetric power relations among participants. In one of these meetings, the chair subtly managed turn-taking and topic control through the use of such devices as passive voice, subjunctive forms and choice of pronouns. In the second meeting, an Agricultural Extension Officer interfered in the process, almost taking over the role of chair. The chair's speech consisted of a number of presequences, false starts, changes in word order, direct speech and choices of tense, as she systematically regained control of the meeting. The author concludes that studying the talk that takes place in meetings can provide significant insight into the viability and functioning level of an organization. Further, by analyzing the communication behaviour that actually takes place in a particular setting, appropriate communication training programs can be developed to increase efficiency, effectiveness and feelings of belonging among participants.

Marjan Huisman (2001) studied the interaction and linguistic forms that characterized decision-making in meetings at four Dutch organizations. He uses the expression talk-in-interaction to describe the collaborative construction of decisions, which he concludes consists of three elements. First, participants recursively formulate situations and actions across past, present and future on their way to developing a commitment to future action, which shapes the prospective future of the organization. Second, what counts as a decision depends on the specific composition of the group involved and the norms that the members have established in working together. Finally, consideration must be given to the subjective, situational and interpretive characteristics of the way in which scenarios are formulated. For example, individuals may present information selectively, they may alter their level and form of participation depending on the circumstances, and they may interpret information differently depending on how it is presented and how it fits with their own perspective.

In a study based on transcripts from the Language in the Workplace database, Janet Holmes and Meredith Marra (2004) examine the ways in which leaders manage conflict during meetings. They observed that leaders employed four different strategies that ranged across a continuum with respect to level of confrontation. From least to most severe, these strategies were: conflict avoidance, diversion, resolution through negotiation and resolution by authority. Drawing on a fairly conventional categorization of management tasks and responsibilities, the authors conclude that leaders adopt a conflict management strategy that allows them to strike a balance between their transactional and relational goals.

Related to the situational characteristics discussed above, Asmuss and Svennevig (2009) point out that the talk taking place at meetings can be mediated by the existence of written documents, such as agendas, reports, background information, budget sheets, financial statements, as well as various procedural manuals, codes of conduct, by-laws or other regulatory documents. While the content and usefulness of many of these instruments is discussed more fully in the next section, these documents can constrain what is said and decided, provide a convenient hiding place for those not wanting to speak, demonstrate level of preparation, serve as a means to credit or discredit certain participants and contribute to the orderly handling of business.

The findings in these studies might lead us to imagine that the social order that emerges in meetings is entirely negotiated in the process of meeting, even though the structural elements remain fairly constant from meeting to meeting. As was stated earlier in outlining the symbolic interactionist perspective, people respond to things on the basis of the meaning those things have for them. Thus, we should recognize that within the bounds of predictability, and level of control, each occurrence of a meeting will take shape in a way that reflects the situation and circumstances of the time. However, the relative structural isomorphism of organizations, and commonality of events, like meetings, taking place, means that we can say a great deal about what should or should not take place. The articulation of what we might refer to as patterns of expectation has led to the development of rules for meetings that, while external to the collective consciousness of the participants, still manifest themselves in a way that reflects how they are understood.

Rules of Order

> Even in the absence of any formal directive it is of the utmost importance that the basic rules of order be understood and observed; otherwise participants are made unsure of their rights and limitations, controls are weakened, and the authenticity of decisions may be open to question. (Stanford 1977: 63)

This succinct and definitively expressed statement from Canadian parliamentarian George Bourinot (1836-1902) captures the essence of rules of order, as well as the primary justification for their existence. They facilitate the establishment of the greatest possible degree of certainty and conformity, what we might otherwise call shared meaning, in what we have seen to be the highly uncertain and negotiated context of meetings.

Particularly as meetings took on a more formal structure and function, rules of order were established with the intention of aiding efficiency and effectiveness in human interaction. At the simplest level these rules were designed to introduce a standardized framework, so that energy could be expended in the accomplishment of business rather than in constantly having to redefine and renegotiate how things would get done. The best known example of rules for meetings is *Robert's Rules of Order* (2011), which is devoted to outlining how items of business are to be introduced into a meeting and how participants are to handle those items, in order to reach a decision and attain a level of confidence that once a decision has been made it will be accepted as settled and, consequently, acted upon.

Among the most important elements discussed in *Robert's* is the idea of an agenda. Without a plan, the potential exists for meetings to go in any direction, or no direction at all. With an agenda, participants know what to expect and the chair, the person responsible for steering the meeting and ensuring that participants are treated fairly, has a template against which to judge whether the meeting is on course or not. Further, the agenda signals two critical transitions—moving from not being in a meeting to being in a meeting, and from being in a meeting to not being in a meeting. As obvious and trivial as these transitions may sound, their proper implementation can have a significant impact on the quality of a meeting and on the way in which participants will evaluate meetings.

Borrowing a phrase from Garfinkel (1967), in their examination of meetings in the video editing department of a large computer company, Arnulf Deppermann et al. demonstrate "the irreducible situatedness of the constitution of action" (2010: 1715). They suggest that even when a previously established and agreed upon agenda exists and participants orient their interactions around that agenda, the actual reciprocal construction of what takes place in the meeting is an emergent and, to some extent, unpredictable phenomenon. Each action that takes place in the meeting gives rise to a number of possible next steps, with the actual sequence of events being determined by who chooses to respond, and how they respond, at any given moment. The authors observe that deviance from the proposed, or expected, course of events takes place incrementally, rather than constituting a clear-cut or deliberate breach. Thus, the actual accomplishment of the agenda is a function of the way in which the participants collectively interpret and respond to what arises in that particular situation, under the circumstances at that time.

Similarly, Mie Femo Nielsen suggests that the format of a business meeting is "an interactional achievement requiring intense collaboration" (2013: 34). Based on her analysis of transcripts from seventeen meetings held in various departments at four separate companies and a trade union, she describes the ways in which meeting participants collectively make the transition from gathering for a meeting to actually being in a meeting (openings) and from being in a meeting to moving on to other pursuits (closings). Alternately, these transitions can be described as passing from the informal to the formal and the formal to the informal (Atkinson 1982).

Nielsen identifies five techniques that are used to open meetings: two by participants and three by chairs. Participants open meetings by showing readiness or passing opportunity to talk. Chairs open meetings by using a boundary marker, making reference to procedure or making a start declaration. With respect to closing techniques, the author identifies two used by participants and four by chairs. Participants either show readiness to close a meeting, or they pass the opportunity to speak. Chairs engage in topic bounding or preclosure, make concluding remarks, issue a last call for matters to be considered or declare closure. One aspect to highlight about these techniques is the parallelism between the methods of opening and closing—the only difference being the act of summarization made by the chair as part of closing.

Based on a survey of 665 individuals who regularly attended meetings as part of their work, Steven Rogelberg et al. (2013) describe meetings as a key component in the temporal activity of organizations. Meetings can consume a large portion of the work-day, they can interrupt or punctuate workflow and they can serve as markers of the passage of time (e.g., weekly staff meetings). Further, meetings can provide a basis for evaluating the quality of time spent at work, as well as the quality of any particular meeting event. Finally, meetings can be a focal point of lateness. They showed that 37 per cent of the 331 meetings reported on started an average of about fifteen minutes late. Through their analysis, the authors found that lateness can have a significant negative impact on the quality of group decision-making, the well-being and stress of employees, interpersonal relationships, power and deviance, withdrawal and overall organizational effectiveness.

The existence of rules of order is no guarantee that meetings will either run more smoothly or accomplish more or better results. At the same time, it is critical to recognize that, like a strange attractor, rules of order exist to pattern behaviour, rather than predict and control what takes place in a meeting. Despite this, critics of rules of order suggest that they may actually impede rather than facilitate proceedings. In some cases, this reticence reflects the fear that someone who knows the rules will use that knowledge to control proceedings. Should collective ignorance form the basis for abandoning standard procedure, or is this yet another example of confusing epistemology with axiology?

Some critics have even gone so far as to create alternate systems of what might be referred to as anti-rules of order, in which reaching consensus replaces the formality of discussing and then voting on an issue (Susskind and Cruikshank 2006). These authors define consensus as reaching an "overwhelming agreement" among members, not necessarily unanimity, as means of "overcoming the tyranny of the majority" that is the consequence of following parliamentary procedure. They outline five essential steps in their consensus building approach:

Convening

Assigning roles and responsibilities

Facilitating group problem solving

Reaching agreement

Holding parties to their commitments (2006: 22)

On the face of it, it is difficult to see how these steps differ in any significant way from the procedures outlined in RRO. On closer examination, however, the undemocratic and manipulative nature of this scheme becomes clear. For example, the convening process involves identifying interested parties, meeting with them beforehand to determine their motivations, going through a selection process to ensure that the right people come to the table, and then proceeding to bring people together on an issue only after the convener has reached an acceptable level of confidence that the selected individuals will commit to their positions and carry out necessary actions. This sort of "stacking the deck" is a primary example of the sorts of behaviours that rules of order were designed to prevent.

Another approach to overcoming the perceived difficulties with RRO is the construction of a sort of hybrid arrangement designed to strike a balance between formality and participative democracy (Urbaniak 2011). Much of what is presented in Urbaniak's book is a primer on the fair and just application of rules of order, rather than an actual rewriting or abandonment of RRO or Bourinot. A key component of his argument is the need for participants to be better informed and more committed not only to the matters brought before an assembly for discussion and decision, but to the details of the process used in meetings.

Better Meetings

To close out this chapter, here is some advice from one of the best-selling books on how to remedy problems with meetings. Patrick Lencioni, in his aptly titled *Death by Meeting* (2004), suggests that there are two primary problems with meetings. First, meetings are boring because they lack conflict. Individuals running meetings tend to focus on avoiding tension and getting through the agenda in a timely manner, without ever allowing for varied opinions to be expressed, developed and adequately analyzed. Second, meetings are ineffective because they lack contextual structure. Even with an agenda, participants are often unclear about what the objectives of specific meeting are. Are they being asked for their opinion, their assent or are they just there to listen and nod sagely?

As a remedy for these ills, Lencioni outlines four different kinds of meetings that should take place. First, daily check-in meetings, which should only last for five to ten minutes, allow workflow to be monitored, small hiccups to be addressed before they develop into full scale problems, and help to maintain a personal relationship between managers and employees. While this sort of meeting could take place in a manager's office, it is an ideal means for practicing what is known as management by wandering (walking) around, which entered public consciousness when it was featured as an exemplary practice by Tom Peters and Robert Waterman in their book, *In Search of Excellence* (1982). Second, weekly tactical meetings, which should last for about one hour, should be designed to focus on operational matters within a unit or department. The emphasis here is on the details of the business and getting the job done. Third, monthly strategic meetings, which can run for two to four hours, are meant to provide an opportunity to discuss a small number of issues in greater detail and to focus on long-term concerns and opportunities. Finally, quarterly off-site review meetings can last for one or two days and, as the name suggests, should be held in a location away from the regular workplace. The purpose of these meetings is to review performance, examine what is happening in the industry, provide adequate time for interaction among staff members, and to accommodate staff development activities. The reason for holding these meetings off-site is to ensure that participants are not drawn back into the day-to-day details of running the business—a definite shut-off-your-smart-phone situation.

These four types of meetings highlight the relationship between content and timeliness. As people carry out their daily activities, certain aspects of what they do—and how they view what they are doing—need to be monitored and examined on a frequent basis, while other aspects can be reinforced and reviewed much less often. This is critical to the establishment of good governance and maximizes the potential for leadership to emerge. The recommendation for daily meetings recognizes the priority of maintaining human relations, a big part of which is related to the fact that certain elements of people's lives change rapidly, unpredictably and with significant consequence. The weekly tactical meetings focus more on the collective, recognizing the need for social feedback and for reinforcing feelings of belonging and shared understanding and responsibility. The monthly strategic meetings provide an opportunity to revisit the overall driving force—motivation, goals and objectives—that inform an organization's existence and operations. Unlike the weekly meetings, which look at the current status, monthly meetings look to the future. The off-site meetings represent the need to step outside the immediate and familiar environment, in part, because physical space and surrounding technologies can have a huge influence on what people think and what they are willing to say. Context can contribute to the maintenance of existing ideas and ways of doing things. A change in context opens up the possibility for new ideas and practices to emerge.

Another important aspect of meetings to take into consideration is the activities that take place both before and after the actual meeting. In a number of pre-meetings and post-meetings, key points of discussion, strategies and the establishment of common understanding are often worked out among selected subgroups of participants. This is a natural and productive aspect of group behaviour and, contrary to the suggestion of Susskind and Cruikshank, it should not be manipulated or controlled. If it is, people will just find another mechanism through which to accomplish it. As one might anticipate, meetings outside of the meeting usually take place in an alternate venue, such as a hallway, coffee shop or parking lot. While to some observers unofficial and informal encounters may appear subversive, they are often critical to the success of the meeting and many times are the primary mechanism through which shared understanding is accomplished, thus facilitating the transformation of ideas into action.

7. Understanding Leadership

Though the subject of leadership is often treated as a separate and distinct area of learning and expertise within organizational management studies, it is critical to remember that all leadership takes place within some sort of governance framework. Those involved in any sort of collective social enterprise may not be explicitly aware of the exact nature of that framework, but it will be there nonetheless. Furthermore, while appropriate governance structures can facilitate the emergence of needed and constructive leadership, an inappropriate governance structure can fail to prevent the emergence of detrimental or destructive leadership. In some instances, the governance structure may actually prevent leadership from emerging at all. A more detailed analysis of governance is provided in chapters 9 and 10, but for now our attention will be focused on what gets talked about in discussions of leadership.

Management and Leadership

As a starting point, our efforts to understand leadership will be greatly facilitated by acknowledging the fact that much of what currently falls under the guise of leadership is really more properly designated as management. The two phenomena are related, but the ways in which they are conceptualized, and the dividing line between them, has shifted significantly in the last couple of decades. In part, this state of affairs has come about because global society now finds itself in a constant crisis mode, characterized by ethnic conflict, terrorism, natural disasters and a plethora of economic and environmental tragedies attributable to human error or greed. At the same time, this shift is associated with a certain debasement of the occupation and practice of management, as reflected in the title of an insightful article by Jackie Ford and Nancy Harding, "Move over management: We are all leaders now" (2007). Among other things, these authors advocate for a shift away from thinking in terms of how leadership can contribute to organizational performance to questioning whether the established ways of thinking about leadership are legitimate or efficacious.

Looking more directly at what constitutes these two activities, one familiar distinction concisely and perhaps too cleverly states that management is doing things right, while leadership is doing the right thing. The expression *things right* carries with it the notion of correctness in execution, aligned with a readily determined course of action, while the expression *right thing* implies a more fundamental ethical view, which recognizes the possibility that there is a choice to be made between various alternative courses of action, whether based on epistemological or axiological assumptions. Expressed another way, management may be viewed as pertaining to how things get done, blended of course with ensuring that they do get done, while leadership is about what gets done and what happens if things do not get done.

The practice of management is based on a tangible set of skills that can be taught, learned, practiced, done well or done poorly. Its tasks can be delineated, and positions reflecting the appropriate scope of authority, responsibility and accountability can be designated with a reasonable degree of specificity. Leadership is none of these things.

Having said that, the apparent objective and tangible nature of management should not be interpreted to suggest that it is not messy. In fact, it is likely the case that the messiness of management is the thing that comes as the greatest shock to many newly appointed managers. They did not enter management to deal with seemingly peripheral, and extraordinarily time-consuming, personal and personnel matters. They wanted to take on greater responsibility and advance their careers. They wanted more money, more prestige and more power. Similarly, what many managers and executives fail to recognize in their quest to climb the corporate or political ladder is the harsh reality that the higher you are positioned in the organizational hierarchy, the more bosses you actually have, in the form of board members, shareholders, industry watchdogs and the public. The idea of social leadership captures this seeming paradox.

In one of the first efforts to formally describe management, French mining engineer Henri Fayol (1841-1925) proposed that it consisted of six functions: forecasting, planning, organizing, commanding, coordinating and controlling (1949). These functional categories reflect Fayol's analysis of industry around 1900, and as such there is an emphasis on production related concerns, with very little consideration of the human side of the enterprise. Based on his observation of executives at work, Henry Mintzberg (1973) constructed a ten-part taxonomy of management roles divided into three categories that account for all of a manager's activities. Under the heading of information processing, he includes the roles of disseminator, monitor and spokesperson. In the category of decision making, he includes entrepreneur, disturbance handler, resource allocator and negotiator. Finally, under the category of interpersonal activities, he lists liaison, figurehead and leader. According to Mintzberg, the emphasis on one or the other of these roles will be dependent on the circumstances and situations faced by the individual manager, and there is a significant degree of flexibility with respect to how these roles will be carried out. While Mintzberg's taxonomy identified those roles common to all managers, some researchers, such as Rosemary Stewart (1982), suggested that certain aspects of management would be specific to particular types of organization. Stewart analyzed management in terms of the demands, constraints and choices impinging upon and available to managers, and suggested that management behaviour would reflect the pattern of relationships and the pattern of work in the organization, as well as the exposure related to particular actions. The idea of high exposure, for example, reflects actions with important and highly visible consequences that could have an impact on an organization's operations or reputation.

As the use of the term management as a collective expression covering a range of functional elements has been increasingly replaced by the use of the term leadership, management has been divided into a number of distinct specialties, such as human resource management, operations management, strategic management, information systems management, change management and so on. To some extent this move reflects the fact that the complexity of these functions has increased, but it also reflects the trend toward the professionalization of work (Abbott 1988). No one wants to be a mere employee or worker, and as the number of more traditionally defined management (higher ranking) jobs is limited, and seemingly declining, the alternate path toward more money and increased prestige is to become a professional. As a consequence, the much neater, and more directly measurable, realm of task management has eclipsed the far messier and arguably more challenging realm of relationship management.

If management is a pervasive and ubiquitous aspect of the normal operation of organizations of all kinds, then leadership should be viewed as a latent and rare phenomenon that only emerges when the circumstances are right. As was alluded to above, in any particular setting, there are likely to be many instances when leadership is required, but it does not emerge.

In what is probably the most concise and yet most comprehensive book available on the study of leadership, Brad Jackson and Ken Parry state that when it comes to studying leadership: "You can actually attempt to lead, you can observe leadership in action, you can talk about leadership, you can read about it and you can write about it" (2011: 1). Of course not everyone will have the same opportunity to engage in any or all of these approaches. In part, what the authors are trying to capture in this statement is the idea that there is no one best way to go about increasing your understanding of leadership. At the same time, they are pointing out that learning about leadership does not necessarily have to take place in a formal setting, under the direction or guidance of experts. Even a casual conversation at the dinner table or while waiting in line for your latte can provide valuable insights into this much discussed and little understood phenomenon.

As elusive and yet desirable as an adequate understanding of leadership may be, there is no denying the fact that we have a tendency to overestimate its importance. James Meindl and his collaborators (1985) refer to this phenomenon as the romance of leadership. These researchers discovered that when there was no direct or unambiguous evidence to indicate otherwise, people attributed organizational outcomes to leaders. This was especially the case in extreme situations where either great success or utter failure occurred. As Jackson and Parry point out, in these instances: "leadership acted as a simplified, biased and attractive way to make sense of organizational performance" (2011: 52). Meindl (1995) further suggests that opinions about leaders are socially constructed by followers. Part of the explanation for this behaviour can be attributed to social contagion—the way in which ideas and opinions spread like a virus among interpersonal networks and groups. Similarly, the amplifying effect of media coverage can both shape and influence public opinion about leaders, as both heroes and demons make for valuable news content.

Evidence of this process can be found in the "celebrity CEO" phenomenon (Guthey et al. 2009). It is difficult to think about Richard Branson, for example, without at the same time thinking about the Virgin brand, and all of the positive and negative connotations associated with it, and therefore with him. Similarly, think of the once revered domestic icon Martha Stewart who fell from grace when she was found guilty and jailed for insider trading, and then remarkably had her image and her empire redeemed and reconstructed after her release. Bill Gates of Microsoft, who was often demonized for the stranglehold that the MS-DOS and then Windows operating systems had over the personal computer industry, was transformed into a paragon of social consciousness thanks largely to the influence of his wife Melinda, who got him engaged in a number of philanthropic projects. The social cachet of the Gates family and its charitable foundation rose even higher when they recruited Warren Buffet, chairman and CEO of Berkshire Hathaway—widely acknowledged as the world's most successful investor—to their cause.

Describing the romance of leadership phenomenon from a somewhat different perspective, Hans Hansen et al. suggest that leadership "became the great dumping ground for unexplained variance" (2007: 544). In other words, when researchers could find no other explanation for the changes they discovered while measuring various aspects of organizational performance they attributed these changes to leadership. While this practice may have the effect of making leadership sound both mysterious and of great importance, above all else it demonstrates that leadership has not been adequately conceptualized. Instead, leadership researchers appear to be falling back on two largely discredited explanatory practices, more commonly found in theology—the "god of the gaps" and the *via negativa*.

The expression "god of the gaps" has its origins in the work of Scottish evangelist Henry Drummond (1851-1897), who chastised Christians for attributing to God, anything that science (the systematic application of reason to the interpretation of evidence) could not yet explain. The key word here is *yet*. As the corpus of scientific knowledge grew, and arguably continues to grow, there is less and less about the universe and everything in it that required an explanation outside of science. Drummond's point is that the current absence of a definitive scientific explanation for some phenomenon does not justify positing a supernatural one in its place. The recent discovery of the Higgs boson, or so-called "God particle," demonstrates not only the staying power of this disingenuous piece of intellectual *legerdemain*, but also suggests the equally fallacious conclusion that there is little if anything of any great consequence remaining for science to discover—the last gap has been filled.

The *via negativa*, or apophatic approach (reasoning by denial), is a method developed by scholastic theologians to describe an indescribable God in terms of what God was not. In other words, based on the assumption that God was transcendent, any characteristic that could be adequately described was therefore not attributable to God, because God had to be beyond description. Consistent with this method, scholars and pundits began to define leadership in terms of what it was not rather than in terms of what it was. If something could be explained, it was not leadership. If something could not be explained, and in many cases this was something destructive, harmful or unethical, then it was called leadership. The fact that the use of the word leadership has increased significantly over the last decade or so suggests not only that instances of exceptional organizational performance, positive or negative, have increased, but that our ability to understand these instances has correspondingly decreased. At the risk of placing organizational studies on a par with theological speculation, we must admit that, if the concept of leadership is to be retained at all, it is in desperate need of adequate and appropriate conceptualization.

What the Experts Say

Starting at the practical end of the spectrum, if you are going to learn about leadership, for whatever purpose, what are the things that you should learn, and how should you go about learning them? Of course, any answer to this question has to be predicated on the acceptance of the idea that leadership is something that can be learned, and therefore taught. We will take that as a given, for now. As mentioned at the outset, standalone texts on leadership emerged out of the literature on organizational behaviour and management. Consequently, the material for this section is drawn primarily from two of these standard sources (Daft 2011; Yukl 2013), both of which have gone through several editions and are used extensively in business schools.

Both books are directed primarily at preparing individuals to assume roles of responsibility and power in the corporate world. Both are about the same length (just over 500 pages), and both have a highly structured chapter format. One (Daft) makes extensive use of visual aids, including magazine-style glossy paper, background colours, multiple font sizes, colour diagrams, sidebars, icons and irregular page layout—perhaps of great appeal to a younger generation, but for me a dizzying and often illegible experience. The other (Yukl) has a more consistent, formal and, in my view, fitting appearance for a text that is designed to exhibit both authority and accessibility, with consistently-sized black type on white paper, uncluttered line diagrams and distinct margins.

While these texts reflect the ways that leadership is taught in business schools and professional administration programs, they contain much of the same material that would be presented at an internal or company-sponsored leadership training session, with a few significant differences. First, for the purpose of offering instructors some flexibility in course design, the texts contain far more material and fine detail than could be comfortably and adequately covered in a single course. Second, they are heavily documented with citations to scholarly books and articles, both as a means of appropriately acknowledging sources and as a way to provide interested students with resources for further study. And finally, they condition almost everything they present by indicating the extent to which any particular element has or has not been subjected to adequate empirical testing, suggesting that those ideas that have not been adequately tested should be viewed as hypotheses or educated guesses rather than facts.

Training sessions, on the other hand, which are generally restricted in duration to a few hours or a couple of days, tend to focus on a single topic, or are aimed at developing a particular skill. Similarly, as they are designed for practitioners, these sessions focus on the practical (immediately useful) aspects of being a leader rather than on the theoretical and more strictly academic fine points. Furthermore, unlike what takes place in the classroom, much of the time spent in training sessions is consumed in environmental adaptation—getting coffee, checking out the room, assessing fellow participants, evaluating the instructor and figuring out what bar to go to afterwards for the socially mandatory, and often more rewarding, debriefing session.

Following a brief introductory chapter that looks at the nature of leadership and the reasons for studying leadership, Richard Daft (2011) divides the remainder of his text into four sections. The first of these examines research perspectives on leadership, and is divided into two chapters, the first of which deals with traits, behaviours and relationships, while the second explores various contingency approaches to leadership—theories that view the phenomenon as a quid pro quo. The second section explores the personal side of leadership over four chapters. The first of these focuses on the individual in terms of personality, values, attitudes and cognitive differences. The second one deals with leadership mind and heart—expressed as the difference between competence and capacity. Next, issues of morality and courage are dealt with. Finally, attention is shifted toward the role of follower and the nature of the relationship between leaders and followers.

The third section shifts to more of an action orientation, with an emphasis on the leader as a relationship builder. The five chapters in this section cover motivation and empowerment, leadership communication, leading teams, developing leadership diversity and leadership power and influence. The common thread among these topics is they are on the human side of the organization. The final section, while still retaining an action orientation, shifts the focus toward the organizational level, viewing the leader as social architect. The topics covered here include creating a vision and strategic direction, shaping culture and values and leading change. The common thread throughout the entire text is the recognition and advocacy of the ontological supremacy of the leader.

Gary Yukl (2013) does not divide his text into sections. Rather, he covers much of the same material as Daft over sixteen chapters that do not appear to be arranged in any particular order. Rather, his chapters tend to start by outlining a particular theoretical perspective and then looking at how that perspective can be evaluated and applied. So for example, in the Daft text, charismatic and transformational leadership are introduced as examples of theories based on power and influence. In the Yukl text, these theories, both of which have received a great deal of scholarly attention, are treated together in a chapter devoted to them. While it might be an overstatement to suggest that the Yukl text takes a more academic approach, its structure reflects the way an academic is likely to think about leadership, whereas the Daft text is more clearly focused on using academic material to support the deliberate and systematic training of leaders.

Both texts include cases studies at the ends of chapters that can be used as teaching instruments in the classroom, as group projects for presentation or as individual assignments to evaluate progress in understanding and applying key concepts. Business cases are supposed to be detailed accounts of real organizational events usually involving decision making, based on first-hand collection of data, and approved for educational use by someone in the organization (Mesny 2013). The case study method was developed at the Harvard Business School over one hundred years ago and has become a standard element of business program pedagogy. The method is defined by four characteristics: direct and collective student involvement in in-class discussion, facilitation by the instructor, the primacy of the particular over the general and the targeting of learning goals in the cognitive, affective and practical domains (Christensen and Hansen 1987). As with anything to do with education, irrespective of the level, the method has its avid supporters and its detractors.

One of the main criticisms leveled against the method is that the cases fail to reflect the reality of organizational management. Anne Mesny reports on a study by Neng Liang and Jiaqian Wang (2004) of sixty-six of the most widely used Harvard cases, in which they find that "MBA cases emphasize reason over emotions, economics over politics, material benefits over intangibles and meanings, and strategy formulation over organization building" (2013: 60). Further, critics have questioned whether in fact there is active participation and engagement on the part of the students, or whether instructors are overly directive, or come to dominate discussion in order to make the best use of time, or stress a particular point. There are also some who question whether the case method actually counts as experiential learning. Are students acquiring managerial skills that can be transferred to their work life?

The case method has for the most part squeezed out alternative approaches to learning and student assessment. Not only does this method perpetuate the Harvard hegemony over what constitutes a valid business school education, it also tends to be based on an oversimplification of circumstances and too often serves to substitute the application of standardized analytic techniques for the development of a deep and lasting understanding of theoretical principles. Whether in the context of business schools, the workplace or community organizations, active teaching is still an essential part of genuine learning, and acquiring a certain level of understanding of foundational concepts should precede efforts to apply them.

Given the emergent and highly contextual nature of leadership, it is difficult to imagine what benefits would accrue from using the case study method as a means of developing either an understanding of leadership or a stock of leadership skills.

Elsewhere, Yukl presents a hierarchical taxonomy of leadership behaviours (2012: 68), starting with the lowest order aspects, as follows:

Task-oriented
- Clarifying
- Planning
- Monitoring operations
- Problem solving

Relations-oriented
- Supporting
- Developing
- Recognizing

- Empowering

Change-oriented
- Advocating change
- Envisioning change
- Encouraging innovation
- Facilitating collective learning

External
- Networking
- External monitoring
- Representing

This scheme reflects many of the items identified by Fayol and Mintzberg as integral to management, and includes the two traditional realms within which management and leadership skills and theories are often described; namely, task orientation and relationship orientation. It supplements these with two additional realms, one of which (orientation to change) can be viewed as a concern for time (beyond the now), and the other (external), which brings in the dimension of space (beyond the here). Consistent with a relational approach, these skills are largely expressed in a gerundial form. These are not behaviours that individuals identified as leaders will necessarily carry out, nor would the practice of these behaviours necessarily result in leadership emerging. Rather, these are behaviours that one would hope are engaged in by all members of an organization, thus contributing to the social conditions in which leadership has the potential to emerge and be responded to.

What People Want

What do people want in a leader? Do our expectations reflect our genuine assessment of the situation and circumstances in which we are operating, or have we been conditioned to expect certain things from a leader without really knowing why, or if those things are really going to be of any benefit? Scholars refer to our preconceived notions about leadership as implicit leadership theories (see Offermann et al. 1992), and they originate with our parents, our teachers, our communities and such factors as the television programs we watched and books we read when we were young. Anyone who has taught leadership will likely tell you that these preconceptions are extremely difficult to overcome or replace no matter how much knowledge or experience a person accumulates. Rather than trying to replace these assumptions, some approaches to understanding and teaching leadership start by discovering what these notions are and then building on them.

Over the past three decades, and through five editions, Jim Kouzes and Barry Posner (2012) have created one of the bestselling books on leadership (more than 2 million copies sold), and from it a popular training program, complete with study guides, workbooks and a variety of audio-visual support materials. Through an ongoing survey that includes respondents from Africa, North America, South America, Asia, Europe and Australia, they have identified the most sought after characteristics of leaders. The top four are:

Honest

Forward-looking

Competent

Inspiring

Other items on the list, in decreasing order of popularity, include: intelligent, broad-minded, fair-minded, dependable, supportive, straightforward, cooperative, determined, courageous, ambitious, caring, loyal, imaginative, mature, self-controlled and independent (2012: 34). Even limiting our attention to the top four, can you imagine any way of training people to develop these characteristics? Kouzes and Posner give it a try.

In their book, they identify five practices and ten commitments, each of which is broken down into a series of specific actions. The five practices are:

Model the way

Inspire a shared vision

Challenge the process

Enable others to act

Encourage the heart

Each of these practices is further divided into two commitments.

Model the way:

- Clarify values by finding your voice and affirming shared values.
- Set the example by aligning actions with shared values.

Inspire a shared vision:

- Envision the future by imagining exciting and ennobling possibilities.
- Enlist others in a common vision by appealing to shared aspirations.

Challenge the process:

- Search for opportunities by seizing the initiative and looking outward for innovative ways to improve.
- Experiment and take risks by constantly generating small wins and learning from experience.

Enable others to act:

- Foster collaboration by building trust and facilitating relationships.
- Strengthen others by increasing self-determination and developing competence.

Encourage the heart:

- Recognize contributions by showing appreciation for individual excellence.
- Celebrate the values and victories by creating a spirit of community.

As with the material examined in the previous section, all of these items are likely to be viewed as things that we would like to see all members of an organization engaging in. All of them can help to create a greater capacity to act, and all of them can be viewed as placing relationships ahead of entities. The fact that they are broken down into a convenient ten-point scheme makes them easy to remember, and it certainly facilitates the construction and delivery of modular training programs. But, none of them actually amount to leadership, nor is it at all clear how any of these actions will help a person to become honest, forward-looking, competent and inspiring. Rather, on closer examination, these characteristics appear to be prerequisites for the actions suggested. Cause and effect have traded places.

As part of their delivery method, Kouzes and Posner weave narratives drawn from real-life situations into their explication of principles. On the face of it, this sounds like a reasonable and useful thing to do. In some sense these accounts resemble small case studies, presented in fragments to punctuate and give a conversational and informal feel to the text. Here is a short excerpt from one of the stories:

> For example, when Samieh Bagheri became a new manager, she needed to learn how to motivate and inspire her new employees. She was young and dedicated, and wanted to do more in her job. At times she probably took on more than she was ready to handle. (2012: 224)

Storytelling has an undeniable appeal, and there is no question that it is helpful in the learning process when people can identify with someone who is experiencing the same sorts of challenges and anxieties that they are. One can almost visualize the reader nodding in recognition and sympathy, as the narratives unfold. However, stories like these raise a couple of red flags. First, even this short excerpt demonstrates a tendency toward pop psychologizing and paternalism. Second, these accounts bear a striking resemblance to what Rudyard Kipling (1865-1936) referred to as "just so" stories, in a book by that name (1902). Kipling used these stories to explain to children how certain things came to be as they are; for example, how the leopard got its spots, or how the alphabet was made. In a more technical sense, the term has come to represent unverifiable narratives with popular appeal. Such stories can have the effect of lulling readers into a false sense of certainty regarding their understanding of a concept, while at the same time building within them a false hope that they will obtain the same result should they apply what they have learned from these stories in their own situations.

At the risk of appearing to be too harsh and even a little hypocritical in this criticism of the authors' methods, it reflects a broader concern that, especially when it comes to writing about leadership, we have a tendency to engage in excessive infantilization—sadly an ubiquitous phenomenon (Porterfield et al. 2009). Whether it is a matter of thinking that the subject is too difficult for people to understand or whether we are trying our best to allay anxiety, many of the leadership books aimed at the general reader are remarkably guilty of this sort of condescension and pandering.

Top Ten Lists

The seemingly insatiable quest to understand and become better at leadership is well represented by the endless stream of new books that are published on the subject. A general search on Amazon. com using the keyword leadership returns more than 116,000 results, while a search limited to books with the word leadership in the title returns more than 46,000 items (as of early 2014). Common sense would suggest that they all cannot be saying the same thing, or the number would logically be much smaller. At the same time, it suggests that, while opinions abound, there is little or no consensus on what leadership is, or how best to describe it. That being said, some of those who study leadership are willing to identify what they consider to be exemplary contributions.

Jackson and Parry provide, somewhat melodramatically, and with what I suspect is at least a hint of sarcasm, their list of "ten leadership books you should read before you die" (2011: 152-53).

The list includes:

Improving Organizational Effectiveness through Transformational Leadership. (Bass and Avolio 1994)

Leadership. (Burns 1978)

On Leadership. (Gardner 1990)

Servant Leadership: A Journey into the Nature of Legitimate Power and Greatness, 25th anniversary edition. (Greenleaf and Spears 2002)

Leadership: Limits and Possibilities. (Grint 2005)

Clearings in the Forest: On the Study of Leadership. (Harter 2006)

Leadership without Easy Answers. (Heifetz 1994)

The Leadership Challenge, 4th ed. (Kouzes and Posner 2007)

Rethinking Leadership: A New Look at Old Leadership Questions. (Ladkin 2010)

Leadership for the Disillusioned. (Sinclair 2007)

The authors do not provide a detailed rationale for their selection, and space does not permit providing even the briefest summary of what these books have to offer. However, a few observations can be made. First, not all of these books represent recent contributions, and so we might wonder what new insights have we gained over the past few decades? Second, a few of the titles emphasize not only the fragility, incompleteness and mistakenness of our knowledge, but they also reflect the extent of our perplexity over our seeming inability to say anything constructive, let alone definitive, about leadership.

For the purpose of comparison, this next list was put together by the Garza brothers on the Empowerment Network (www.asdfasdf.com). Here are their top ten:

The Art of War. (Sun Tzu 2002)

Losing My Virginity: How I Survived, Had Fun, and Made a Fortune Doing Business My Way. (Branson 2011)

The 21 Irrefutable Laws of Leadership. (Maxwell 1998)

The Prince. (Machiavelli 1958)

Primal Leadership: Realizing the Power of Emotional Intelligence. (Goleman 2002)

Leadership is an Art. (DePree 1989)

Man's Search for Meaning. (Frankl 1962)

Why Leaders Can't Lead: The Unconscious Conspiracy Continues. (Bennis 1989)

The Age of Discontinuity: Guidelines to Our Changing Society. (Drucker 1992)

The 7 Habits of Highly Effective People. (Covey 1989)

At first glance, at least, this list appears to reflect a more positive evaluation of the state of our knowledge, and a couple of titles even suggest that there are some specific actions that individuals can engage in to improve their leadership skills. The list also digs back deeper into history, with *The Art of War*, which was written at least 1,500 years ago, and *The Prince*, which was written about 600 years ago. It also includes texts that represent what might be viewed as being at opposite ends of the spectrum. Richard Branson's autobiography extolls the virtues of independence and unlimited potential, while Frankl's autobiography speaks directly to the way in which people from different walks of life can come together in the face of extreme adversity and work together not only to survive, but to reinforce each other's humanity.

As a reflection of my aversion to reductionism, I am not going to offer my own list of the ten best. However, I am willing to offer some suggestions for reading, based on what I have read and on some books and types of literature that many others have read. First, I think that reading the classics is always a good thing, so while I would recommend Machiavelli and Sun Tzu, I would also add the Bible and the Qur'an. I include these sacred texts not because I am trying to give expression to any sort of particular religious conviction, but rather because the influence of these texts over several centuries and in the lives of billions of people is unparalleled by any other written works. With respect to newer books, as will become clear in the final two chapters of this book, I am a big fan of Greenleaf and DePree (especially when it comes to the evolution of my own ideas). From a more formal foundational point, I started with Peter Drucker's *Management: Tasks, Responsibilities, Practices* (1973), and then Tom Peters' and Robert Waterman's *In Search of Excellence* (1982).

However, I have never found non-fiction works, whether aimed at an academic or popular audience, to provide the greatest insights into the nature of leadership, or into the nature of the human condition more generally. Rather, I have learned more by reading literary works, especially from authors like Hermann Hesse (see Chapter 11), William Shakespeare (d. 1616), Franz Kafka (1883-1924) and Dr. Seuss (1904-1991).

With respect to the latter three authors, Shakespeare's works stand out not only for the tremendous insight they provide into power, intrigue and human frailty, but because of the form in which they are written (plays) and for their masterful display of language, in all its clarity, nuance and ambiguity. Kafka, as a pioneer of existentialism and surrealism, highlights the absurdity of formal social arrangements, especially bureaucracies and legal systems, and the way that personal identity is a fragile and constantly re-negotiated phenomenon.

Theodore Geissl (Dr. Seuss) contributes a different sort of absurdity—one marked by a curious brand of humour and extensive wordplay (my personal favourite example being *If I Ran the Circus*, 1956). His works reflect the unfettered imagination of a child, and yet they exhibit tremendous sophistication and insight, even though he wrote them within the confines of a particular rhyme scheme (primarily anapestic tetrameter) and with a limited vocabulary. In fact, one his best-known books (*The Cat in the Hat*, 1955) came about in response to the challenge from his publishing company of only using a 250-word vocabulary—he ended up only using 236.

The works of these literary authors, and undoubtedly many others, demonstrate the essential tension between agency and structure, and the ways in which real life plays out as an expression of freedom within boundaries. The dynamic reciprocity and complementarity of these phenomena is what the concept of social leadership is meant to capture.

8. Studying Leadership

Leadership Research

This section focuses on scholarly approaches to leadership, with an exploration of both the theoretical and methodological aspects of academic research. While the sheer number and variety of theoretical models of leadership can come as a surprise to many readers, the unity and conformity of the methodological approaches are equally noteworthy. Given the lack of consensus regarding the nature and definition of leadership, the theoretical diversity can be easily explained. One would assume, however, that, by this same logic, there would be an equally diverse array of alternative and potentially complementary approaches to examining leadership in the field. Surprisingly, this does not appear to be the case.

Samuel Hunter et al. (2007) describe the typical leadership research project as one that relies on the administration of a survey for the purpose of gathering data and on the analysis of that data using statistical techniques to test hypotheses and generate conclusions. More specifically, these surveys are often pre-developed tools, such as the multifaceted leadership questionnaire (MLQ; Bass and Avolio 1990), that have been administered in multiple studies, and therefore are assumed to provide a valid basis for comparison and refinement. In most instances, surveys are distributed to employees who self-report their assessment of their immediate supervisor's behaviour. In some studies, these same instruments are administered to managerial and supervisory personnel to report on their own behaviour. The survey results are then correlated with an outcome measure, such as organizational performance, which is also determined through self-reporting. The authors point out that this approach is based on a number of assumptions about the nature and role of subordinates, leaders, context and process, that may be unwarranted.

With respect to subordinates, one of the key assumptions that the authors expose is that simply by asking questions about the leadership behaviour of their superiors, researchers are assuming that these individuals possess an innate need or desire for leadership. In fact, the exact opposite may be the case. Individuals may carry out their duties within an organizational setting, collaborating with peers or working as sole professionals, viewing the role of management as one of obstruction or interference. Second, administering the same survey instrument in multiple settings presupposes that the particular work environment and the exact nature of the employees and the work they carry out are not relevant factors. Further, we have no way of knowing if subordinates have had the opportunity to witness the full range of leadership activities or behaviours in which their superiors engage. Managers may engage in a very different suite of behaviours with their subordinates, than they do when they are interacting with their peers or the individuals who they themselves report to. Finally, given the amount of supervisory, management and leadership training that takes place in all sectors of the economy, it is difficult to imagine that those respondents completing a survey would not have had some exposure to the ideas being studied. This lack of respondent naïveté can significantly distort results, as some individuals attempt to respond in the way that they think the researchers want them to, while a few others may even do the exact opposite.

Perhaps the most damaging assumption that these studies make regarding leadership is to equate managers with leaders. Just because someone holds a management position, or is in charge of something or someone, does not mean that they are a leader—someone who is actually demonstrating leadership. Further, studies tend to focus on the positive side of leadership, rather than examining the ways in which an individual's behaviour can be harmful to their subordinates or their organizations.

Looking at the survey tools themselves, there is an assumption that they are psychometrically sound. In other words, researchers fail to question whether in fact these instruments are measuring the right things, and whether those measurements actually tell us what they think they do. Further, our faith in the objectivity and statistical accuracy of these instruments prevents us from questioning whether they are able to capture the most critical and essential aspects of a leader's behaviour—whatever those might be.

Furthermore, so-called method bias seriously hampers many leadership studies. Method bias includes such elements as an over-reliance on the use of standardized surveys, a lack of inclusion of appropriate control variables, and the extensive use of same-source variable assessment. This latter phenomenon can be described as a situation where the opinions of subordinates are used for the measurement of both independent and dependent variables. In other words, the researcher creates a situation where the conclusion that a certain factor leads to a particular result becomes largely self-evident, or at least self-fulfilling, because the source of information regarding that factor also provided information with respect to the related result. As an illustration of just how deleterious method bias can be, Hunter et al. point out that in one study (Brown and Keeping 2005) the researchers found that as much as 32 per cent of the variance could be explained by how much the subordinate liked their supervisor (2007: 439). While this sort of finding may provide some insight into human nature, it tells us precious little about leadership.

Two other elements that generally receive inadequate coverage in leadership research studies are the influence that social context has on the actual practice of leadership and the dynamic nature of leadership. Because the vast majority of leadership studies provide a snapshot of what is actually taking place, frozen in time, they are unable to provide any information about the processes of leadership. Similarly, because individuals interact with a large number of others, including coworkers, clients, as well as other supervisors and managers, the assumption that the act of leadership is restricted to the relationship between that individual and a particular leader misses much of what actually takes place. Leadership cannot be conceptualized strictly as a one-on-one, or dyadic, event. It is difficult to imagine that the particular actions of the leader are the sole or most critical cause of a certain response in subordinates. It is equally difficult to conceive of the situation where what takes place at a specific point in time is the principal cause of a particular response. More likely, and more consistent with people's experience, is the assumption that individuals respond to a cumulative perception or interpretation of a situation based on a number of discrete experiences over a given period.

At the risk of cavalierly dismissing the cumulative work of many dedicated, talented and well-intentioned researchers, there are exceptions to the rule—but they remain exceptions. The homogeneity of approaches to leadership research is an example of institutional isomorphism, as discussed in Chapter 4. As is the case for academic researchers in all disciplines, if leadership scholars want to have their work funded and published, and if they want to secure their future careers, they must conform to the standards of the field. However, the standards of the field have become that way, not on the basis of what researchers have accomplished by following them, but rather on the basis of the sheer volume of research activity that has taken place in accordance with them—what De Bono (1971) would call recognition rightness.

Review of Academic Approaches

Despite all of the research that has been carried out, Jackson and Parry suggest that: "hard evidence about the impact of leadership is surprisingly and tantalizingly hard to find" (2011: 7). Yet, this has done nothing to diminish our fascination with it. In their survey of the enigmatic and immensely popular field of leadership studies, these authors point out some of the deficiencies and explore promising trends in leadership research representing five alternative theoretical perspectives, those that are: leader-centered, follower-centered, cultural, critical or based on a higher purpose.

Regarding the leader-centered perspective, the authors open their discussion with a brief review of the two approaches that have, and to some extent still do, dominate research and popular opinion on leadership; namely, trait-based theories and behaviour-based theories, which respectively link leadership to who you are (leaders are born not made) and what you do. While these approaches have largely been discredited, or at least surpassed, within the context of scholarly efforts to understand leadership, their fundamental appeal to our conventional ways of thinking has allowed them to maintain considerable influence, especially in the media.

One aspect of these approaches is the study of the role of gender as a determining factor in leadership effectiveness. While this line of inquiry has attracted a good deal of attention, it has failed to produce conclusive results. Jackson and Parry suggest that perhaps this failure should be interpreted as a sign that we are asking the wrong questions. To illustrate their point, they highlight two interesting observations. First, they mention the phenomenon of the "glass cliff" (Haslam and Ryan 2008), whereby women are appointed to leadership roles under conditions of increased risk of failure or criticism. Reflecting two aspects of gender bias, researchers have suggested that these appointments are made on the assumption that women are better suited to dealing with these sorts of situations, and that these situations provide excellent opportunities for women to showcase their skill and potential. Anecdotal evidence for this phenomenon can be found, for example, in the cases of Carly Fiorina at Hewlett Packard, Kate Swann at W. H. Smith and Patricia Russo at Alcatel-Lucent. Second, a multinational study found that individuals, whether female or male, who made it to the top of the corporate ladder were able to do so because they had the luxury of having someone else to look after their domestic concerns, which for many women meant not having a husband and/or children (Neale 2001).

One approach that has dominated leadership research since the 1980s is transformational leadership, a theory that includes the "conception of the leader as someone who defines organizational reality through the articulation of a vision, and the generation of strategies to realize that vision" (2011: 31). One of the first things to understand about transformational leadership is that it is closely coupled with transactional leadership, which is based on the idea of an exchange relationship between a leader and a follower. For many advocates of newer approaches to the study of leadership the ideal situation is when both of these forms are used together. So, from the outset, these theories suffer from the problem of lack of independence, in that they rely on the coexistence of more conventional and utilitarian formulations of leadership. More broadly, transformational theories concentrate too heavily on the behaviour of top leaders, while ignoring the significance of both the informal aspects of leadership and context. As Jackson and Parry point out, factors like technology, industry structure, the international trading environment, national public policy and social and cultural transformation, may significantly restrict the actions of leaders, whatever vision they may have (2011: 34). The authors are astounded that this perspective on leaderships still holds so much sway. One possible explanation might be found in the prevalence of the romance of leadership idea. We like to think that leaders create captivating visions and possess the wherewithal to transform our lives.

Charismatic leadership is often viewed as similar to transformational leadership, but it is more likely to be mentioned with respect to leaders in the community, show business, the media or the political environment. The notion of charisma refers to the special quality, or aura, of the leader—magnetic, vibrant, awe-inspiring, somehow larger than life. In their study of the Enron crisis, Dennis Tourish and Naheed Vatcha (2005) identify three characteristics of charismatic leadership: the promotion of a compelling vision, individual consideration and the promotion of a culture characterized by conformity and the penalizing of dissent. Not all cases of charismatic leadership necessarily lead to bad results—Martin Luther King and Mahatma Gandhi stand out as excellent positive examples. However, the notion of charisma is readily associated with self-promotion and narcissism (see Maccoby 2000), as illustrated by individuals such as Richard Branson, Donald Trump and, of course, Adolf Hitler and Vladimir Putin.

The idea of bad leadership, while popular in the media, has not received adequate scholarly attention. Following Barbara Kellerman (2004), Jackson and Parry point out that failing to introduce students of leadership to the negative side of the phenomenon is a great disservice. Not only may they be misled into thinking that all leaders are for the most part well-intentioned individuals out to do good things for an organization, when they encounter the opposite, they are likely to be confused and ill-prepared to cope with the situation.

As a counterpoint to the idea of bad leadership, the notion of leaders who started out as good and became great has had significant influence on the way we think about leadership, as witnessed by the tremendous success of *Good to Great*, by Jim Collins (2001). In this book, Collins identifies what he refers to as "level 5 leaders," who work behind the scenes, having no need for the limelight, and who are quick to give credit to others. Just as the lack of attention to bad leadership likely reflects our desire to think that it is a rare occurrence, our over-attention to the type of individual characterized by Collins demonstrates our ceaseless yearning for model leaders. However, wishing does not make it so. These individuals are likely to be much rarer than their counterparts.

With respect to follower-centered perspectives, most theories about followers appear to represent a mismatch between their ontological and axiological assumptions. From the point of view of causality, it is followers that make leaders, to the extent that in the absence of followers, there is no one to lead. At the same time, the role of follower is usually presented as second best, even though this is the role that most people will find themselves in throughout their life. Some newer approaches are shifting this perspective. For example, Boas Shamir (2007) suggests that followership is a complex and varied role, in which followers may be recipients of leader influence, moderators of leader impact, substitutes for leaders, constructors of leadership, or as leaders themselves. Jackson and Parry add a sixth role, envisioning followers as co-producers of leadership.

One of the best known theories of followership is the so-called situational leadership model (Hersey and Blanchard (1977). This model suggests that leaders must adapt their style to match the maturity level of their followers. While this model recognizes that followers contribute to the construction of leadership, it still places followers in a secondary and largely passive role—it merely suggests that processes of influence and manipulation need to be tailored to match individual recipients of leadership. In contrast, the servant leadership model, which will be discussed at length in Chapter 11, shatters the traditional ontological ranking and causal relationship between leaders and followers, and posits a more collective conception of leadership that places axiology ahead of ontology.

Concluding their discussions of follower-centered perspectives, Jackson and Parry draw attention to a view regarding education expressed by Dennis Tourish et al. (2010), that

> business schools should abandon their obsessive promises to produce transformational leaders and begin presenting an alternative and more realistic prospectus based on enlightened followership and the promotion of effective upward communication within organizations in order to create healthier and ethical organizations. (2011: 67)

Expanding this message beyond business schools and into the way that we prepare individuals to participate in every facet of collective social action is consistent with the notion of social leadership.

Cultural approaches to leadership have been linked primarily to the notion of organizational culture and the importance for leaders to create and maintain a culture that is consistent with the overall goals and objectives of the organization (see Schein 2010). In contrast, Jackson and Parry cite Lynn Meek (1988), who remarked that "most anthropologists would find the idea that leaders create culture preposterous: leaders do not create culture; it emerges from the collective social interaction of groups and communities" (2011: 73). These divergent views continue to be explored.

At the same time, there has been a shift toward examining the effect that people who represent different national and ethnic cultures have on the practice of leadership. This shift is associated with the globalization of business and politics and the need for leaders, and others, to develop their cultural intelligence—characterized by knowledge of culture, mindfulness and a corresponding repertoire of behavioural skills (Thomas and Inkson 2004). Recent research efforts have been directed at building the requisite bank of knowledge to support the development of this new sort of intelligence.

Geert Hofstede (1980) pioneered this research in the late 1970s, identifying four dimensions that differentiated management and leadership practices in different countries: individualism versus collectivism, power distance, uncertainty avoidance and masculinity versus femininity. After further research in the 1980s, he added a fifth dimension: long-term versus short-term orientation. While Hofstede's research has been criticized for being poorly designed, under-theorized, and outdated, it still forms the foundation for the majority of studies in this area. Other researchers have modified or expanded upon these dimensions, for example, with the introduction of the linguistic versus emotional dimension (Hall and Hall 1990), which identifies the contrast between the use of low context languages like English, that is literal and direct, and high context languages like Arabic, that is more ambiguous and subtle.

In the late 1990s, a far more systematic and extensive research initiative known as the Global Leadership and Organizational Behavior Effectiveness (GLOBE) project was carried out by 127 investigators (House et al. 2004). These researchers surveyed 17,300 middle managers, working in 951 organizations, in 62 societies, compiling a massive amount of data that has still not been fully analyzed. Through their efforts, they identified nine major attributes of culture: future orientation, gender egalitarianism, assertiveness, humane orientation, in-group collectivism, institutional collectivism, permanence orientation, power concentration, and uncertainty avoidance. What impact, if any, these attributes might have on the way that people operate within organizational settings has yet to be adequately explored.

Recognizing that cultural studies of leadership are still a relatively new phenomenon, Peter Dorfman (2003) has identified four caveats for those who would engage in this sort of research. First, we must recognize that the culture within any country or ethnic group is not unitary. There may be many subcultures, even in a small geographic area, or among members of a small subpopulation. Second, even within a relatively unitary culture, or subculture, an observer may see radically different expressions of some element of that culture, all of which are considered, by those practicing them, to be correct and integral to social identity. Third, and related to the previous point, there may be a broad range of understanding and adherence to various aspects of culture on the part of individual members of that culture. Finally, elements of culture and the ways in which they are expressed are in a constant state of flux. Tradition can be a strong social force, but everything changes.

Those theories of leadership that Jackson and Parry refer to as representing critical or distributed perspectives are concerned with concentration of power among a few select individuals. First, critical theories challenge conventional hegemonic views of power, replacing them with a more relational view, such as that of Michel Foucault (see 1977), who emphasized that the true nature of power is most evident when it is exercised. In this regard, they draw attention to what Erving Goffman (see 1961), in reference to asylums and prisons, referred to as total institutions. These bodies, which have the power of incarceration, broad-ranging rules and surveillance, represent an extreme form of bending the will of people to the will of the organization—a dehumanizing effect that all organizations, to some extent, share. Critical theories focus on identifying the mechanisms through which power is abused—they have been less focused on offering solutions.

Second, distributed theories view leadership from the perspective of process and therefore place the roles of leader and follower into a secondary position. Among the theories in this category are: co-leadership, shared transformational leadership, distributed leadership, leaderless work groups and team leadership. This array of theories reflects a diverse set of supporting assumptions. For example, one version of shared transformational leadership, known as upper echelons theory (see Hambrick 2007), holds that leadership is essential to organizational performance and is best shared among senior executives with complementary skills. Alternately, Jackson and Parry point out that one of fundamental assumptions of distributed leadership is that, while individuals possess inherent leadership capabilities, "organizational forms must be made less bureaucratic in order to liberate that leadership potential" (2011: 103).

The final perspectives discussed by Jackson and Parry are those that view leadership as being grounded in a higher purpose, such as altruism, integrity or a guiding spirit. Part of the reason these approaches are receiving more attention is because of the heightened awareness and concern with morality and ethics that has accompanied the seeming increase in corporate scandals and financial malpractice. The authors point out that there are those who think that part of the blame for these immoral and unethical activities resides with business schools that traditionally place financial success and greed above all other considerations (2011: 114).

Two of the prominent approaches to leadership that fall into this category are authentic leadership and spiritual leadership. Just what constitutes authentic leadership can be difficult to define, but the authors point out that, according to Kernis (2003), authenticity has four components: "a full awareness and acceptance of self; an unbiased processing of self-relevant information; action consistent with the true self; and a relational orientation that values openness and truth in close personal relationships" (2011: 117). On one level, this approach might appear to reflect the romance of leadership perspective. At the very least, while perhaps reflecting our deepest desires, it represents a sort of idealism that is unlikely to manifest itself in the real world of business, politics and collective action.

The notion of spiritual approaches to leadership represents two related, but quite different, understandings of the way in which people go about living their lives. The first, and possibly least controversial, version is associated with the idea that people have a spiritual side, which needs to be nourished, and which influences our actions and relations. Being in harmony with nature and possessing a holistic vision of human action are typical characteristics of this sort of approach. Second, and perhaps more controversial, are those approaches that could more correctly be classified as religious. These perspectives are informed by a pre-existing set of beliefs originating in a specific religious context, whether Christian or otherwise, and therefore include such elements as a transcendent and authoritative being (god), a code of ethics and a plan not only for how people should behave, but for what the consequences will be for either following or deviating from that plan.

The authors also introduce a series of lesser known approaches to leadership that, while perhaps not directly linked to the notion of a higher purpose, at least reflect efforts to understand leadership in ways that stand apart from conventional—and what some might consider legitimate—perspectives. Pragmatic leadership, for example, emphasizes a back-to-basics approach that focuses on the very practical and seemingly mundane elements of the day-to-day lived experiences of those involved not only in the corporate environment, but also in communities and society, more generally. While we have already looked at the issue of aesthetics, these authors emphasize that researchers are beginning to view it as an essential part of leaders arsenal of skills, along with technical ability and ethics.

Under the heading of sense making and the art of leadership, the authors introduce a number of sources from the fine arts (e.g., painting), martial arts and performing arts (e.g., dance, theatre) that leaders can draw upon to help people understand their organization differently and potentially stir creativity. Related to this, they draw attention to the use of metaphors for leadership, e.g., leadership as parenting, leadership as schooling and leadership as captaincy.

Jackson and Parry mention the practice of having participants in training sessions write haiku to express key principles in learning leadership and project management (2001: 128). Studying master works of poetry is also likely to provide considerable insight into the practice of leadership, as illustrated by this piece—*Ozymandias* by Percy Bysshe Shelley (1792-1822).

> I met a traveller from an antique land
> Who said: Two vast and trunkless legs of stone
> Stand in the desert. Near them, on the sand,
> Half sunk, a shattered visage lies, whose frown,
> And wrinkled lip, and sneer of cold command,
> Tell that its sculptor well those passions read
> Which yet survive, stamped on these lifeless things,
> The hand that mocked them and the heart that fed:
> And on the pedestal these words appear:
> "My name is Ozymandias, king of kings:
> Look on my works, ye Mighty, and despair!"
> Nothing beside remains. Round the decay
> Of that colossal wreck, boundless and bare
> The lone and level sands stretch far away.

Putting aside your vague, and likely bad, memories of being forced to memorize works like this in high school, pretend for a moment that these are pearls of wisdom scattered by some big name leadership guru. What does this poem say to you? The next time you want to devote a few hours to leadership training for the members of your organization, hand out a copy of this poem and let people talk about what it means to them, and think about what the organization might learn from the collective wisdom of those interpretations.

To close out their book, Jackson and Parry identify four priorities for future research: "complexity leadership theory; the linkage between leadership and identity; the relationship between leadership and governance processes; and understanding the sources as well as the prevention of destructive leadership" (2011: 148). Two of these issues are especially relevant here, with one topic, understanding the relationship between leadership and governance processes, obviously constituting the major thrust of this book. The other topic, complexity leadership theory, is examined in more detail in the final section of this chapter.

Locus and Mechanism

Morela Hernandez and her collaborators (2011) examined the full spectrum of leadership models as a precursor to developing a common language through which leadership models could be compared, contrasted and generally discussed in a constructive manner. Rather than focusing on methodological issues and the types of evidence that researchers used in support of their ideas, the authors categorized models in terms of the ways in which they addressed the questions of where leadership comes from and how it is transmitted. Based on their findings, they constructed a two-dimensional grid that located models in terms of the assumed locus and mechanism of leadership.

With respect to the locus of leadership, the authors discovered five potential sites: leader, context, followers, collectives and dyads. Even though these loci are placed on a grid for visual representation, they are not to be seen as existing along a continuum. They are independent categories, and while certain theories take more than one locus into account, for the most part the majority of theories focus primarily on one. There are a few exceptions, with one model, leadership complexity theory, being viewed as equally distributed across the leader and context foci. Regarding the foci themselves, a few points of clarification are in order. The authors use the term followers in this instance to suggest that leadership originates in the actions of followers, as distinct from notions of followership, which describe followers solely from the perspective of following. The notion of collectives suggests the actions of a network or team of individuals, in the absence of distinct roles of leader or followers. Dyads refer to situations where a leader develops one-on-one relationships with each individual follower. The idea of context is interesting because it places the source of leadership outside of specific individuals and instead highlights the importance of situation and circumstance, as well as cultural and environmental factors.

The four mechanisms are: traits, behaviours, cognition and affect. As with the loci, these mechanisms are considered to be independent of each other—not located along a continuum. More models appear to straddle more than one mechanism, than was the case with multiple loci. Leadership complexity theory, for example, covers behaviours, cognition and affect, although cognition is seen as the primary mechanism. Conceptually, the four mechanisms are based respectively on who you are, what you do, what you think and what you feel. The authors point out that the mechanism of affect has received the least attention among researchers.

From a philosophical perspective, the assumptions about locus and mechanism represent two aspects of ontology, with the former referring to the primary entity involved, and the latter referring to the way that causation takes place. Irrespective of which locus is selected, leadership theories place one of these at the top of the ontological hierarchy and develop a causal chain from there. Despite the resulting ontological incompatibility of models, the authors suggest that our understanding of leadership is best served by being open to insights from all perspectives. The purpose of their classification scheme is not to exclude certain models based on difference, but rather to provide a common vocabulary that allows for constructive conversation across differences. In terms of specific recommendations, the authors suggest that theories of shared leadership (Pearce and Conger 2003) and strategic leadership (Hambrick 2007), both of which to this point have been discussed in terms of a limited number of loci and mechanisms, show the greatest potential for future research across the full range of ontological options.

Complexity Leadership Theories

Leadership theories that attempt to incorporate insights regarding the behaviour of complex adaptive systems are an inevitable development out of the recognition that ideas about governance and leadership associated with General Systems Theory are no longer adequate. They can also be viewed as a response to other emerging trends associated with the advent of the Information Age (see Riordan and Hoddeson 1997), such as social media, and the transition to a knowledge society (see Stehr 1994) or knowledge economy (see Drucker 1999), as represented in the recent championing of "big data" analytics (see Davenport and Kim 2013).

In response to these developments, Mary Uhl-Bien et al. (2007) outline the fundamentals of a Complexity Leadership Theory (CLT). They suggest that CLT recognizes three types of leadership. First, administrative leadership represents the traditional form of leadership associated with hierarchical and bureaucratic organizations, with its emphasis on command and control. Second, the term enabling leadership is used to describe the activity of establishing structures that support creative problem solving, adaptability and learning within an organization. Finally, they use the term adaptive leadership to capture the idea of leadership as a "generative dynamic" that both informs and is an integral part of changes as they emerge in the organization. This tripartite leadership scheme appears to be hierarchical and evolutionary, moving from administrative through enabling to adaptive. Similarly, in terms of complexity, the administrative type seems contrary or in opposition to complex operations, the enabling type can be viewed as supportive and thus, in some sense, causal, while the adaptive type can be conceived as an emergent component of a complex system—an effect of the workings of complex processes.

The authors also suggest that CLT incorporates four critical notions. First, their theory recognizes context as an active component in the construction and operation of a complex system, rather than as an antecedent or constant. Second, they differentiate between leaders and leadership. For them, leaders are individuals who contribute to the establishment of the enabling environment, whereas leadership is something that emerges as part of the system dynamic. What this separation of concepts appears to suggest is that leaders are not doing leadership. Rather, they are primarily facilitators of leadership, which may or may not happen, but which, if it does happen, will only do so as a product of social interaction in specific circumstances and situations. Third, and partially in recognition of the distinction just made, they separate the activity of leadership from its association with managerial positions, or those holding particular offices. Finally, they emphasize that leadership will only emerge in the face of adaptive challenges requiring learning, innovation and new ways of doing things, rather than in the face of technical problems or situations where the application of existing methods and practices will suffice.

9. Governance, Hierarchies, Markets

Defining Governance

L ike the concept of leadership, which has become a catch
basin for a broad range of ideas and ideologies, the notion
of governance is shrouded in ambiguity and misunderstanding.
On the one hand, it is commonly confused with the concept of
government, and thus can generate an evaluative response; we
view it as irreparably intertwined with the rhetoric and manipulation of the political process. On the other hand, it is often subject
to an equally restrictive interpretation, being limited to discussions of corporate boards of directors and boards of governors in
not-for-profit contexts. In this view, it can be seen as elitist or
hegemonic, reflecting concerns with secrecy, control and single-
ness of purpose, whether profit oriented or philanthropic. Neither
of these perspectives, however, captures the full range of meaning
and significance of governance processes.

To begin with the most fundamental distinction, Mark Bevir
points out that: "Governance differs from government in that it
focuses less on the state and its institutions and more on social
practices and activities" (2012: 1). Governments govern, but so do
corporations and every other form of social organization engaged
in establishing and maintaining parameters under which collective social action is carried out or subverted. As such, governance

needs to be understood as referring to the variety of situation specific rules of engagement through which social interaction takes place.

Given this broader understanding of this phenomenon, scholars have tried to capture its essence through a range of alternative conceptual frameworks. For example, Bevir takes a jurisdictional approach, exploring the categories of organizational governance, corporate governance, public governance, global governance and good governance. This latter category introduces an overarching axiological component to his discussions and some of the points he raises in this regard will be examined at the end of the next chapter under the heading of sustainability governance. The three primary forms of organizational governance identified by Bevir (hierarchical, market and network) provide the structure for this chapter and the next. In what follows, corporate governance is discussed under the heading of policy governance and public governance is examined along with network governance. A brief introduction to global governance is provided after this introductory section.

Examining the phenomenon from a more structural perspective, Andreas Duit and Victor Galaz (2008) postulate four types of governance: rigid, robust, fragile and flexible. They developed their typology specifically in response to the challenge of governing within environments that are best described as complex adaptive systems. The four types are characterized on the basis on how well they support the processes of exploitation and exploration. The former refers to the capacity of an organization to build on existing resources and ways of doing things, while the latter deals with the capacity to carry out activities that are innovative, experimental or responsive to changes, whether generated internally or externally.

Rigid governance structures, which are typical of conventional bureaucratic forms of organization, are those with high capacity for exploitation and low capacity for exploration, and thus are best suited to perpetuate the status quo and focus on stability. Robust governance structures possess high levels of capacity for both exploitation and exploration, but specific examples of organizations with this form of governance are difficult to identify. Fragile governance structures are at the opposite end of the spectrum from robust structures, in that they possess low levels of capacity for both exploitation and exploration—a characteristic of the governments and regulatory regimes in many developing nations. Flexible governance refers to the situation where an organization has a low capacity for exploitation and yet a high capacity for exploration. This situation can occur when there are multiple participants in a particular venture, but adequate systems of communication and coordination among them are lacking—much like an anticommons. As might be anticipated, the authors suggest that only robust governance structures will have the capacity to support the behaviour of complex adaptive systems.

In an effort to understand the widespread occurrence of governance failure, John Dixon and Rhys Dogan (2002) explore the philosophical assumptions that underpin hierarchical, market and network governance systems. They begin their analysis by referring to the four factors that contribute to governance failure identified by Renate Mayntz (1993). These are: a knowledge problem stemming from a lack of governance know-how, a capability problem associated with a lack of appropriate governance instruments, an implementation problem that leads to a lack of governance effectiveness, and a motivation problem that manifests itself in a lack of compliance by the governed. Dixon and Dogan suggest that the knowledge problems are related to epistemology, the capability and implementation problems are related to ontology and the motivation problems are nomological.

From their perspective, the major dividing line in epistemological debates is between those who advocate for a naturalist perspective and those who support a hermeneutic position. In terms of method, or how a governance system could operate, they suggest that naturalism provides prediction without explanation, while hermeneutics provides explanation without prediction. Ontological positions can be divided among those that posit agency as the primary causal entity and those that view structure as the major determinant of human action. Metaphorically, the authors imagine the causal flow of structure as top-down and of agency as bottom-up. Based on these dichotomies, they suggest that the hierarchical mode of governance is structuralist and naturalistic, the market mode of governance is also naturalistic, but gives primacy to agency, and network governance is structuralist and hermeneutic. Interestingly, they do not identify a form of governance that has its foundations in hermeneutic agency. Social leadership could be viewed as consistent with this fourth option, but an adequate picture of this phenomenon is more complicated than can be captured by dichotomies.

Dixon and Dogan link people's motivation for operating within a particular governance structure as a function of nomology—our expectations about what constitutes the normal and correct way that things should operate. Hierarchical systems are based on expectations about predictability that stems from the individual application of reason. Market systems are predicated on the expectation that participation will result in personal material advantage. Finally, network systems are based on a broader understanding of collective commitments, without necessarily meeting the needs of specific individuals or institutions. The philosophical incompatibility of these alternative systems leads to a situation where efforts to discuss governance result in either an unresponsive dialogue or a "dialogue of the deaf" (2002: 186). The former expression refers to those situations where one voice dominates the conversation (hegemony), leading to an increased polarization of opinion and an increased intransigence on the part of those wielding power. A dialogue of the deaf describes the situation where many voices can be heard, but no one is listening—the United Nations comes to mind.

By way of offering a solution, Dixon and Dogan suggest that the philosophical conditions necessary to support societal governability are an epistemology grounded in critical realism and a structurationist ontology. As discussed in Chapter 3, the structurationist position views agency and structure as complementary rather than as opposites. The critical realist perspective (see Baert

1998) posits that the real world operates on three levels—the actual, the empirical and the deep. The implication of this view is that our knowledge of the world is at best unreliable and incomplete, primarily because our systems of knowledge acquisition cannot deal with either the actual or the deep levels of reality. While these authors do not directly address the axiological aspects of governance, their critical realist structurationist perspective does have implications for the idea of sustainability governance, which will be discussed at the end of the next chapter.

In his discussion of leading change toward sustainability, Bob Doppelt (2010) takes a more functional approach to understanding governance, describing the three things that governance systems (should) do. As he states it,

> governance systems are the three-legged stools that shape the way information is gathered and shared, decisions are made and enforced, and resources and wealth are distributed. These factors shape the way people perceive the world around them, the way they are motivated, and their power and authority. (2010: 96)

He goes on to explain that these three factors are not discrete and independent of one another. Rather, they interact and are mutually influential. Furthermore, the patterns of activity and social interaction that emerge around the three processes (should) reflect the goals and core purpose of an organization.

It has already been stated that the goal of both governance and leadership is the creation, development and maintenance of an organization's capacity to act. That capacity will express itself in terms of information handling, decision-making and resource allocation. Leadership, when and if it emerges, will manifest itself with respect to one or more of these three processes, and it will only do so in an environment characterized by a governance framework predicated on facilitating these three processes.

Global Governance

Emerging out of the field of international relations, the primary assumption that informs the notion of global governance is that rules pertaining to matters beyond the scope of individual nations can be established in the absence of both traditional hierarchical institutions and a singular international sovereign power. Theories of international relations have been dominated by two perspectives—realism and liberalism. Realists hold that sovereign states will pursue their own individual interests at a global level, leading to anarchy and power struggles for political dominance. Liberals are interested in maintaining peace and assisting the spread of trade and social welfare around the world. Consequently, they support the development of international law and the establishment of international institutions such as the United Nations and the International Court of Justice. As Bevir states it: "Global governance seeks not only to prevent and limit war but also to manage the global commons, to promote development, and to regulate global financial markets" (2012: 83).

A theoretical framework known as neoliberalism emerged in the second half of the 20th century in an attempt to adequately describe this broader understanding. Scholars such as Nobel Prize-winning economist Friedrich Hayek (1899-1992) suggested that planning and state action were outmoded and fundamentally flawed courses of action on the international scale. What neoliberals suggested was that the self-determining operation of the free market should replace the traditional focus on planning and that states should concern themselves primarily with upholding the rule of law. As might be expected, the neoliberal view contributed to the emergence and prominence of ideas about globalization, especially with respect to global financial markets and trade. While difficult to define in a precise manner, the term globalization expresses a condition of transnational exchange and interdependence (see Stiglitz 2003). More recently, the concept of globalization has been expanded to include noneconomic issues such as climate change, environmental protection and security—finding an adequate response to global terrorism. This shift in focus has led to the establishment of various partnerships and networks that are composed of not only state actors but also many non-governmental organizations and citizens groups (see Kjaer 2004).

As with an anticommons, the existence of multiple governing bodies all claiming jurisdiction over some object of concern leads to a situation where little can get done. Unlike an anticommons, however, these jurisdictional claims are not accompanied by literal ownership. So, the ability of any given actor to impose their will is a function of political rhetoric, moral suasion and bluster—military mobilization, trade sanctions, curtailment of basic rights, etc.—only held in check to the extent that opposing parties are willing to put forward and then act upon a challenge. The opportunities for leadership to emerge in these situations are many; the actual occurrences of leadership are few.

Policy Governance

As an initial response, readers might associate the term policy governance with the establishment and application of government policy—usually referred to as policy studies. Even though there are many parallels with the material covered here, understanding government policy processes is a much-debated and highly controversial area of scholarly and public interest well beyond the scope of this book. As it will be used here, policy governance can be understood more generally to describe the activity of rule-making or establishing the boundaries and parameters under which an organization will carry out its activities—also known as corporate governance (see Mallin 2009). It can cover a broad range of concerns from stipulating that an organization will not engage in any activities that will pose a threat to local wildlife down to the minutiae of outlining what specific items count as eligible expenses on a business trip. Relevant policies will very often be codified and made available to all members of an organization through manuals and other publications, but they may also remain tacit or known to only a select few.

In a more specific sense, the term policy governance is familiar to members of many organizations as Policy Governance®, a set of guidelines for boards of directors developed in the early 1970s by John Carver (Carver and Carver 1996, Carver and Carver 2006). The so-called Carver model outlines four policy areas that are meant to guide the work of the board, and it is built on the following ten principles.

1. *The trust in trusteeship.* This principle concerns identifying the ownership of the organization and determining how owners can be heard. Carver uses the term moral ownership to describe those situations where the basis of ownership, as is the case for many associations that rely on donors, volunteers or the general public, is not legal, as in a contractual or shareholder sense.

2. *The board speaks with one voice or not at all.* The focus here is on unanimity and singularity in dealing with staff, owners and the public. It does not suggest that differences of opinion will not exist. Rather, it suggests that once a decision has been made all parties will act in such a way as to reflect and represent that decision. Carver recommends the establishment of guidelines for individual conduct coupled with the courteous disregard of those renegades who would choose to operate independently.

3. *Board decisions should predominantly be policy decisions.* Boards should not be directly involved in the operational management of an organization. Rather, their purview is policy, as described below in terms of four areas.

4. *Boards should formulate policy by determining the broadest values before progressing to more narrow ones.* The idea expressed in this principle is that boards should initially establish policies that contain expressions of the overarching values of the organization. Any smaller, more specific, statement of values would then have to be consistent with the broader values already articulated.

5. *A board should define and delegate, rather than react and ratify.* Part of what this principle expresses is the fact that it is better to

know ahead of time that a particular course of action is consistent with an organization's policies. In this way staff time is not wasted in misdirected and unactionable planning and board time is not wasted in micro-management and damage control.

6. *Ends determination is the pivotal duty of governance.* This is another principle aimed at steering board activity away from concern and meddling with operational details. Rather, the board's focus should be on the reasons for the organization's existence.

7. *The board's best control over staff means is to limit, not prescribe.* The objective here is to set boundaries by defining what is not acceptable. It also reinforces the idea that after identifying the goals of the organization, it is the job of staff, not the board, to accomplish those objectives by whatever means is appropriate.

8. *A board must explicitly design its own products and processes.* This principle has to do with what the board expects of itself—how it will operate and how it will evaluate its own actions, as opposed to those of the organization.

9. *A board must forge a linkage with management that is both empowering and safe.* This principle deals specifically with the relationship between the board and the highest-ranking member of the staff—most conventionally the CEO. Each party must trust the other to do what is expected of them, without second-guessing or limiting their sphere of action.

10. *Performance of the CEO must be monitored rigorously, but only against policy criteria.* Finally, it is critical for the board to ensure that operations are consistent with policy. As the CEO is the one tasked with overseeing the work of the organization, monitoring CEO performance is the most appropriate means for doing so. This monitoring, however, must be based on a clearly stated and mutually understood and agreed upon set of criteria.

The four policy areas that are to guide the work of the board are of two types—ends and means. Ends policies are those that focus on the mission of the organization in terms of three components—identifying the intended customers or recipients of the organization's products or services, identifying the benefit or outcome the customers will receive, and determining the cost of providing that product or service to the selected target group. The first of the three means policy areas deals with articulating the governance process—how the board will do its job. The second one, stated as board-staff linkage, clarifies what authority will be delegated to the CEO or management of the organization and how their performance will be evaluated. Finally, executive limitations policies describe the boundaries that senior managers can work within, not from the perspective of what they are expected to do, but what they may not do.

The Carver model has been subject to a fair amount of criticism (see Murray 1997), but only a handful of systematic evaluations. Patricia Nobbie and Jeffrey Brudney (2003) studied a number of nonprofit organizations claiming to be following the Carver model to gauge both the extent of implementation of the model and the performance associated with that implementation. They compared these findings against a broader control sample of nonprofits and a smaller sample of organizations that had been involved in alternative forms of board training. The two major conclusions from this study were that the investment in training and the implementation of a governance model, irrespective of the particular model, have a positive impact on board performance and board member satisfaction, and that CEOs respond positively to operating under the Carver model because, for the most part, it prevents the board from meddling in the day-to-day operations of the organization.

Alan Hough (2002) attempts to respond to a number of criticisms that have been leveled against the Carver model. Among these criticisms are the opinion that management cannot be distinguished from governance, ends cannot be separated from means, the model treats the organization in isolation, it ignores organizational lifecycles, stakeholders are more important than owners, and the model is only for heroic boards and perfect CEOs. The common denominators among these criticisms are first that the model is too idealistic and second that it seeks to dichotomize and partition several areas of collective social action. Hough is clearly an enthusiastic advocate for the model and in the end he suggests that the primary basis for most of the criticisms is a lack of understanding of the model.

From a philosophical perspective, the Carver model appears to be based on a substantialist ontology, with the board and the CEO as the primary entities and the causal arrow originating with the board and ending with the CEO. Epistemologically, the model suggests that relevant parameters can be known and articulated, providing a firm basis for measurement and assessment. Axiologically, clarity and precision take precedence over ambiguity, adaptability, independence and even interdependence—there is a linkage between the board and the CEO, not a relationship. Conclusion—in the Carver model, there is no room (need) for leadership.

While the Carver model may represent an effort to simplify or streamline corporate governance, it parallels other approaches in that it offers its own take on a core governance concept known as principal-agent theory (see Eisenhardt 1989). This theory is based on the notion that the ownership and control of an organization will be separated between the principals (owners), who delegate tasks and responsibilities, and the agents (managers), who carry out those tasks and are accountable for them. For the most part, the application of this theory has reflected the predominance of exchange theory as a means of understanding and providing motivation. Consequently, boards and CEOs devote what might be considered an undue amount of effort on the matter of executive compensation (see Garen 1994), to the exclusion of focusing on governance matters, e.g., policy making. More recently, some progress has been made in moving boards and executives toward a focus on the triple bottom line—profit, people, planet (see Epstein 2008). We will return to this topic at the end of the next chapter and in the first section of the final chapter.

Hierarchies

Hierarchies are the most common form of governance structure found in government bureaucracies, corporations and organizations of all kinds (see Wilson 1988). For the most part, they reflect the dominance of a central authority that has its basis in rationality and law, although, historically, tradition has provided an important justification, as best illustrated in patriarchal systems. The easily recognized pyramidal structure, most obvious in institutions like the military, allows for the efficient operation of command and control, with clear lines of accountability linking well-defined positions that designate individual rank or status. As might be expected, hierarchies work best when an organization has a clear set of goals and a corresponding systematic set of means or procedures through which it will accomplish those goals. In these settings, there will be a complex division of labour and occupational specialization, with a highly ramified structure of management and oversight. As anyone who has dealt with a bureaucracy will be aware, written documents, such as procedural manuals, guidelines, reports and standardized forms, constitute one of the primary outputs, if not outcomes, of the organization's daily activities. Max Weber referred to this rigidity and focus on rationalization—a reason for everything and everything for a reason—as the "iron cage of bureaucracy."

Bevir suggests that, from an economic perspective, hierarchies can be viewed as a response to market failure, in that they provide a means for reducing transaction costs and limiting exposure to risk. Similarly, from a sociological perspective, hierarchies are seen to represent our modern concept of rationality and liberal democracy, in part because they establish such clear lines of accountability on the basis of well-defined responsibilities and relationships. Of course, these same characteristics mean that hierarchies may be unresponsive and inefficient, ill suited to situations where there are no clear criteria for success, such as with organizations engaged in creative pursuits or those attempting to innovate. Ambiguity and flexibility are not consistent with formal rules and well-defined relationships. As a consequence, hierarchical organizations are severely challenged when faced by the need for change or adaptation.

In an effort to explain why and how some individuals will seek to preserve an organization even at the expense of the goals it was established to accomplish, German sociologist Robert Michels (1876-1936) posited the "iron law of oligarchy" (Scott and Davis 2007: 61-62). According to Michels, all hierarchies tend toward oligarchy. In other words, power and control tend to rise up to a select few, who then become preoccupied with self-preservation, leading to a situation where both the goals of an organization and the rank-and-file members of that organization become secondary and expendable. The organization is no longer a means to an end, but rather the end itself.

Alvin Gouldner (1954) referred to the type of bureaucracy described by Weber and Michels as punishment-centered. His own research on what actually takes place in organizations, however, led him to suggest that the governance structure in many organizations could be more aptly referred to as a mock bureaucracy, in which rules are overtly broken or ignored. He also recognized the need for representative bureaucracies, in which multiple interested parties engaged in an open dialogue about the goals and direction of the organization. Looking to the future of the bureaucratic form, Paul Adler and Bryan Borys (1996) refer to a shift toward enabling bureaucracies, characterized by flexibility and transparency, as opposed to coercive bureaucracies, with their emphasis on control and rigidity. The extent to which this new form will take hold, as opposed to representing a mere symbolic change, is an open question.

Significant insight into the irrational and dehumanizing aspects of hierarchies can be gleaned from reading Franz Kafka's *The Trial* (1968), and *The Castle* (1998), both of which deal with the way an individual's fate is determined by the seemingly senseless operation of an impenetrable bureaucracy (see Warner 2007). Randy Hodson et al. (2013) point out that Kafka's novels reflect bureaucracies as "inhabited institutions" (see Dobbin 2009), characterized by the existence of divergent goals, patrimonialism, unwritten rules and chaos. The notion of inhabited institutions draws attention to the informal and potentially deviant behaviour that emerges through the operation of human agency. In a manner similar to Michels' ideas about oligarchic control in organizations, the concept of divergent goals recognizes that various groups will seek satisfy their own interests, often in ways that compete with other groups and which may be in conflict with the goals of the organization. Patrimonialism refers to the existence of personal networks through which access to various privileges and promotions is controlled, well captured in the expression "it's not what you know, but who you know that counts." The notion of unwritten rules parallels ideas about organizational culture, in that they express "the way things are done around here." Managers and workers, for instance, will sometimes come to agreement about what rules need to be followed and which ones can be ignored. In one example from Gouldner's research, safety regulations in a gypsum mine were often ignored in order keep up a certain level of production. Finally, the idea of chaos describes unpredictability associated with the external environment within which an organization operates, populated by competitors, regulatory agencies, professional associations and labour unions. It also includes the influence of internal environmental factors, such as the undesired and unintentional outcomes of normal operating processes, miscalculations in planning and the possibility of intentionally deviant or destructive behaviour.

Markets

At the most basic level, markets represent an arena for the exchange of goods. Buyers and sellers come together to satisfy each other's needs, with a price mechanism regulating the balance between supply and demand, such that equilibrium is established. In contrast to hierarchical structures, markets are decentralized and the players are largely independent of one another. Buyers and sellers deal in impersonal transactions that may be highly episodic. As a consequence, there may be little opportunity for the establishment of social bonds, as individual participants place their trust in the system of market governance (competition) rather than in those parties with whom they do business.

Markets appear to offer a number of practical advantages. First of all, they can provide coordination of activities in the absence of some overriding authority. Second, they eliminate the need for both well-intentioned and well-informed planning—the market is the primary ontological entity, not the buyers and sellers. Third, the competitive nature of markets suggests that less efficient buyers and sellers will be eliminated, while at the same time promoting innovation and the development of more appealing products and services. In moral terms, markets ostensibly provide for the greatest exercise of individual choice.

When it comes to disadvantages, the price mechanism of the market can often disguise significant costs. For example, it can require considerable time and effort to gather relevant information about pricing, to locate potential buyers and sellers, and to negotiate contracts. Markets are also inappropriate when pricing information and competition are absent. With respect to the former, there is no adequate mechanism for determining the actual costs associated with social goods. As for the latter, monopolies and cartels can completely undermine competition. From a moral perspective, there is no way to determine in advance whether the outcome of market exchange processes will match our conceptions of social justice.

Just as hierarchies are likely to represent the most common image of what a governance structure would look like, it is equally likely that people would view markets as something to be governed, rather than as a form of governance per se. Furthermore, if asked how markets are, or should be, governed, most people would probably suggest that it is the logic of capitalism that allows the market to operate.

In his foreword to Umair Haque's, *The New Capitalist Manifesto*, Gary Hamel says this about capitalism:

I'm a capitalist by conviction and by profession. I believe the best economic system is one that rewards entrepreneurship and risk taking, maximizes customer choice, uses markets to allocate scarce resources, and minimizes the regulatory burden on business. If there's a better recipe for creating prosperity, I haven't seen it—and neither have you. (2011: ix)

A rather bold claim, and one that represents a vision of prosperity as highly conflictual—Lord Tennyson's "red in tooth and claw"—and highly stratified—Herbert Spencer's "survival of the fittest." In this view, social welfare and meeting the basic needs of all members of society, let alone providing Bentham's "greatest good for the greatest number," do not appear to be part of the capitalist agenda. So, if capitalism in fact drives the market, is there a way to re-conceptualize capitalism, such that it represents an alternative value system—one that is less focused on capitalists and more focused on the population as a whole? And, if that step is possible, will this new capitalism still provide a foundation for the operation of markets?

Adam Smith used the metaphor of the "invisible hand" to refer to the unintended, but inevitable, positive consequences associated with the operation of the free market. From Smith's perspective, when individuals act in such a way as to promote their own self-interest, those actions will contribute to the greater good of all. Thus, as economists would state it, the market only produces positive externalities—beneficial noneconomic effects. The concept of a free (unregulated) market is at the heart of what would come to be referred to as classical, or laissez faire, economic theories.

As the science of economics developed, classical theory was replaced with neoclassical theories that were based on the idea that individuals make rational choices in the presence of full and relevant information, in order to maximize both utility and profits. These theories assumed the existence of perfect competition leading to inevitable equilibrium. In contrast, so-called neo-Austrian theories recognize that the constant environment of change and unpredictability characteristic of real experience can result in disequilibrium. It may be the case that market disequilibrium is a necessary condition for meeting social needs.

In *Das Kapital* (*Capital*), published in stages between 1867 and 1894 (1930), Karl Marx provided much of the framework by which we conceptualize capitalism, and through which we evaluate both its merits and its failings. Marx's primary concern was the exploitation and oppression of the working class by the owners who engaged in the capitalist means of production. Thus, in contrast to Smith, Marx emphasized negative externalities—private gain leads to social loss.

Leaving aside the historical aspects, the primary characteristic of capitalism is the phenomenon of private ownership and the control over the creation and distribution of good and services associated with that ownership. The operation of a capitalist system includes the accumulation of assets (wealth), the existence of competitive markets and the use (exploitation) of wage labour (see Fulcher 2004). It is generally well accepted now that the operation of the markets creates both positive and negative externalities. Among those issues that are still hotly contested, however, are: what exactly constitutes these externalities, how they should be measured and evaluated, and how (if) they should be compensated for and by whom.

As an advocate of a more holistic approach to economics, Umair Haque calls for a shift to constructive capitalism, a new form of capitalism suited for the economic and social conditions of the 21st century. The goal of this new sort of capitalism is the creation of thick value, which is characterized by sustainability, meaningfulness and authenticity. In place of the traditional business emphasis on competitive advantage, Haque offers up a list of potential sources of constructive advantage (2011: 36).

1. *Loss advantage stems from a value cycle that renews resources and makes waste useful.* This principle replaces the competitive notion of establishing a cost advantage through value chain management.

2. *Responsiveness is the result of fluid, ongoing, many-sided value conversations.* Most companies promote brands based on a particular value proposition. This new approach takes the emphasis off the one-sided production of goods and services, for which a demand is created, and replaces it with the evolving provision of solutions to real problems and needs.

3. *Resilience, an evolutionary edge, is achieved by competing with an enduring philosophy.* This concept replaces the focus on market dominance, often achieved by strategic maneuvers aimed at eliminating competition.

4. *Creativity happens when companies strive to complete market-places, creating new arenas of competition.* This principle contrasts with efforts to hold suppliers, customers and other relevant parties captive in order to prevent competitors from entering the market. Instead of providing more of the same, the goal should be to satisfy unmet needs—to plug the holes in a market.

5. *Difference happens when companies seek meaningful payoffs that matter; when companies produce betters, they literally make a difference.* Part of this notion has to do with providing genuine alternatives to customers, rather than merely copying someone else's product, or engaging in mere cosmetic changes. The idea of producing betters rather than goods also carries with it the idea that products and services will contribute more broadly to social wellbeing.

Highlighting the issue of industrial pollution, Daniel Brook (2001) draws attention to the ongoing tragedy of the commons associated with the normal operation of capitalist enterprises. In contrast to Smith's "invisible hand," Brook suggests that there is an "invisible punch," in the form of negative externalities that are disproportionately distributed among the poor and otherwise disadvantaged populations of the world (2001: 612). Consistent with Hardin's comments about technical fixes, Brook's principal message is that the operation of the free market cannot provide solutions for the problems it has created.

Markets and hierarchies are very familiar structures. The fact that they are so ubiquitous and pervasive suggests that the positive aspects of their existence have been seen to outweigh the negatives, when it comes to supporting collective social action. Even though a reassessment of values may be calling this judgment into question, both of these forms provide a convenient means of articulating structure and function. As a consequence, simplicity, isomorphism and inertia, not to mention the seemingly insatiable hunger for wealth and power, have allowed these structures to dominate and thrive. What actually goes on within these structures, however, may in fact be something quite different from the way we think they operate. The actual dynamics of governance may perhaps be best captured through the description of social networks.

10. Networks and Sustainability Governance

Network Fundamentals

The formal study of networks has its origins in a branch of mathematics known as graph theory (see Caldarelli and Catanzaro 2012). In contrast to our more familiar conception of graphs as a visual representation of the relationship between numerical values plotted on a set of coordinates, graph theory deals with the connectivity between points, irrespective of what the basis for that connectivity is, or what the points represent. Mathematician Leonard Euler (1707-1783) is credited with pioneering graph theory, when he tried to solve the problem of taking a walk around the Prussian city of Königsberg (now Kaliningrad) in such a way as to only cross each of the seven bridges joining the parts of the city once. A more up-to-date version of this problem can be expressed as that of a sales representative attempting to visit all customer locations within a particular geographic territory in such a way as to minimize having to double-back or pass by the same location more than once.

Looking at networks from an ontological perspective, there are two fundamental entities that make up the world—nodes and links. Nodes identify discrete substances and links represent relationships. The diagram below illustrates the simplest of networks, with two nodes, A and B, and a link between them, C.

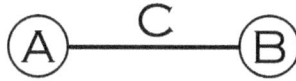

Figure One – A simple network

For the sake of explanation, let us say that this network represents two people who share some form of relationship. From a non-network perspective, typical of most research in the social sciences, we might be interested in looking at the characteristics of the individuals (e.g., age, sex, marital status, education, race, ethnicity, employment status, religion). From a network perspective, however, our focus shifts to understanding the attributes of the relationship (e.g., love, economic dependence, friendship, team membership, business partnership, co-habitation). Not only can there be more than one basis for a relationship, but these bases can vary in strength, and that strength may or may not be symmetrical. For example, two individuals may live together, work for the same company and be friends. However, one of those individuals might consider the other to be their best friend, but the sentiment may not be reciprocated.

Social networks can also differ with respect to size and scale. The former characteristic represents the number of nodes in the network, while the latter represents the geographic distribution of those nodes. One of the powerful attributes of social network analysis is that the same principles can be applied, whether the network consists of a handful of individuals or the entire population of the world. As the number of nodes in a network increases, so does the nature and complexity of the relationships within that network. The following figure illustrates a network with multiple nodes and a diversity of linkages.

The way that connections are formed in networks reflects a number of interesting phenomena, two of which are homophily and triadic closure.

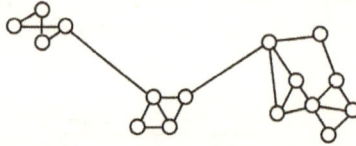

Figure Two – A more complex network

Homophily is the tendency of social entities to associate with others that are similar to them in some way. In a 1954 study, sociologists Paul Lazarsfeld and Robert Merton identified two primary forms. The first type, referred to as status homophily, suggests that individuals of the same age, race, religion, occupation or wealth—to name a few possibilities—are more likely to be in a relationship than individuals who do not share one or more of these characteristics. The second type, value homophily, recognizes that it is also likely that individuals who share similar thoughts or values, such as political views, love of animals, taste in music or tastes in food, among other things, are again more likely to form relationships. A common explanation for homophily is that, in the absence of adequate exposure to alternatives, we go with what we know. In a recent book (2012), sociologist Dhiraj Murthy points out that despite Twitter's ability to easily connect individuals with widely differing thoughts and values, the majority of people still tend to follow others who share views similar to their own.

The notion of triadic closure was originally developed through work on small groups, by sociologist Georg Simmel (see Faust 2010, Nooteboom 2006). He suggested that, if John were friends with Susan and also friends with Bill, then John would exert some amount of effort to ensure that Susan and Bill would also become friends, thus closing the network they form. Researchers use the term transitivity to refer to the assumption made by John that, based on his friendship with both Susan and Bill, it makes sense that the two of them should also be friends. Even though this phenomenon is described in terms of networks with three nodes, it has proven important for understanding the way that networks evolve. Tightly knit networks often emerge as an extension of triadic relationships, while loosely coupled networks tend to exhibit less triadic closure among their nodes. Referring back to the some of the observations made about meetings, if you want to see triadic closure in action, check out the donut shops and parking lots after a meeting.

Along with these aspects of network formation, existing networks display an array of characteristics that can be grouped under the headings of distribution, segmentation and distance.

1. *Distribution*

Distribution in social networks refers to the pattern of connectivity between nodes. It is reasonable to assume that, as overall network size becomes larger, the likelihood that every node in the network will be directly connected to every other node becomes much smaller. Similarly, we should expect that the patterns of disparate connections throughout larger networks would appear more and more irregular. Researchers are interested in discovering what we can learn about collective action from analyzing these patterns. The concepts used to explore network distribution include bridges, structural holes and centrality.

Bridges are connections between sets of nodes (sub-networks) within a network that would otherwise not be connected to each other, or that would be connected through such a long path that the nodes might not even be aware that the connection exists. A simple example would be the case of friendship groups among high school students. A group of students in grade nine is not likely to share friends in common with a group of students in grade twelve. However, if one of the students in grade nine were the younger sibling of one of the students in grade twelve, then that sibling relationship would form a bridge between the two groups.

Sociologist Ronald Burt (1992) suggested that bridges in social networks could be viewed as spanning structural holes—basically empty spaces in the network topology. In a later research study (2004), he demonstrated that managers who constitute nodes at the ends of bridges within organizational networks tend to have earlier access to information, are exposed to alternate viewpoints, have the opportunity to act as gatekeepers and, as a consequence, have greater career success. Burt has suggested in his studies that filling structural holes is a means of building social capital. Looking more specifically at the realm of business, identifying and filling structural holes provides the ideal opportunity for entrepreneurship. As Haque (2011) advocated in outlining a new form of capitalism, instead of competing in a market, the goal should be to complete (fill a hole in) a market.

Centrality refers to the extent to which a particular node plays a central role in a network. Degree centrality is a measure of the number of nodes that are linked to a focal node. Closeness centrality describes how short the paths are between a focal node and all of the other nodes in a network. Betweenness centrality measures the shortest path between any two nodes in the network that pass through the focal node. In terms of capacity to act, being aware of the patterns associated with these different aspects of centrality is key to understanding the way that information will be generated and shared, resources will be distributed and decision-making will take place within an organization.

2. *Segmentation*

Segmentation refers to the fact that social networks are often composed of smaller, more densely tied sub-networks, that may or may not be readily identifiable to outside observers—or even to network insiders, for that matter. Researchers are interested in discovering why and how these sub-networks form and what their impact is on collective action. The relevant topics here include clustering, structural equivalence and cliques.

At the simplest level, the notion of clustering captures not only the fact that ties are unevenly distributed in networks, but that there are often clumps or patches within a network composed of more densely connected nodes. When employees identify which coworkers they speak to on a regular basis on work related matters, or indicate which coworkers they regularly eat lunch with or go for coffee with, they are identifying clusters.

Structural equivalence refers to the idea that, within a large network, patterns of relationship will be shared by a number of individual nodes, such that they appear qualitatively and quantitatively identical. Searching for structurally equivalent nodes involves looking at club membership rosters or purchasing patterns, for example, and identifying those individuals involved. Perhaps the best known example of this approach is Amazon's algorithm for generating book suggestions. If person A buys the following four books (Q, R, S, T) and person B also buys books Q and R, person B will then receive a message indicating that people who bought Q and R also bought S and T. Persons A and B do not have to know each other, nor do they have to provide any information. From a massive database composed of all book purchases (books and buyers as nodes), Amazon can determine the structural equivalence of its customers. The more purchases any set of individuals have in common, the more structurally equivalent they are. This form of analysis could be expanded to cover the full range of products offered by a retailer and could easily be used in a broad range of applications, such as the provision of social services.

Cliques are a special type of cluster that reflect complete mutuality; that is, each member of the cluster shares strong ties with every other member of a small group, normally less than ten people, and more commonly three to five. Cliques represent high-status members of a network, often referred to as the in-crowd. One need only think back to high school for several examples to come to mind. In an interesting historical case, John Padgett and Christopher Ansell (1993) carried out a groundbreaking study of cliques in the patronage network of the Medici family. In a more technology oriented instance, an elaborate analysis of a large international hacker network involved in identity theft and credit card fraud was carried out by a group of information scientists (Lu 2009), who identified thirteen cliques of three to five members each, that acted as central distributors of information and team leaders.

3. *Distance*

The importance of the notion of distance in social networks can be illustrated by the following two questions: If you select two random individuals from a given population, what is the likelihood that they know each other? How many intermediate acquaintances are required to link any two people in a network? Starting out as mere speculation among scholars almost a century ago, researchers have shown that the distance between any two individuals tends to be remarkably short. This so-called "small-world" phenomenon is key to understanding, among other things, the dynamics of viral marketing and the spread of sexually transmitted infections (see Watts 2003).

Stanley Milgram wrote about small worlds in the inaugural issue of *Psychology Today*, in 1967. He was involved in carrying out a number of experiments in which randomly selected individuals in Kansas and Nebraska were asked to get a letter to an individual in Boston, strictly by passing the letter on to someone they thought would have a better chance of knowing the target individual on a first-name basis. Results indicated that it rarely took more than ten steps and, more often than not, it only took about three steps for the letters to reach the target. The popular expression "six degrees of separation," inspired by Milgram's findings, actually comes from a stage play by that name written in 1990 by John Guare, who attributes the use of the particular number six in this regard to a related observation made by the Italian inventor Guglielmo Marconi (1874-1937), in his Nobel Prize acceptance speech in 1909.

Perhaps the most familiar expression of the small world concept can be found in the social media phenomenon of the Bacon number (BN), named after the actor Kevin Bacon (KB). In 1994, three students at Albright College were watching movies together and started to speculate about how many actors had appeared in movies with KB. With the advent of searchable movie databases (e.g., IMDb), it has become a fairly simple process to determine the number of shared appearances between actors.

As an illustration of the game, Kyra Sedgwick, Bacon's wife, has a BN of 1, not because she is married to the star, but because they appeared together in the movie *Lemon Sky*. Mila Kunis has a BN of 2, as she appeared in *Friends with Benefits* with Patricia Clarkson, who appeared with KB in *Beyond All Boundaries*. Finding an actor with a high BN is actually quite challenging, not because of any shortcoming with the technology, but because people tend to be more familiar with so-called A-list actors than they are with the large number of lesser known individuals who fill out the casts of the thousands of films released every year.

According to the authoritative "Oracle of Bacon" website (http://oracleofbacon.org) started by the Albright students, search results indicate that 2,673 actors have a BN of 1, an impressive 292,813 have a BN of 2, and a staggering 968,753 have a BN of 3. As you might anticipate, the numbers dwindle rapidly after that, so that there are just 3 actors with a BN of 9. These results can give rise to the impression that KB is somehow at the center of a vast Hollywood network, but it turns out that similar results emerge irrespective of which actor is used as the focal node.

The use of key individuals to examine distance in social networks has been applied to almost every field of human endeavour. For example, distance in the network of chess players is designated by the Morphy number, linguists have a Chomsky number, economists have a Stiglitz number and, not surprisingly, physicists have an Einstein number. In an effort to better understand the way that a particular organization actually operates, developing a map of the distance between individual employees or members could prove invaluable. Among other things, it would expose the identities of the real key individuals, as opposed to those designated as such by titles and roles.

In a related initiative, sociologist Scott Feld (1991) observed that if you randomly select a group of individuals from a population and ask them to name a friend, the friends turn out to have more friends than the initially selected individuals. The explanation for this peculiar finding, known as the "friendship paradox," is a function of two factors: sampling bias (our tendency to identify extroverts and popular individuals), and the heterogeneous nature of social networks (clustering and centrality). Recognition of the phenomenon has given rise to some interesting research.

Nicholas Christakis and James Fowler (2010) carried out an experiment with university students to monitor the spread of the H1N1 virus, prior to the release of a vaccine. A few hundred individuals were randomly selected from the student body and they were each asked to identify a friend. The date of onset of the flu among members of the two groups (initial contacts and friends) was then recorded. Within a few days of starting the experiment, the researchers observed that members of the friends group were contracting the virus in greater numbers than the initial contacts.

This trend continued over a 46-day period until the epidemic reached its peak. One of the significant implications of this experiment is that it suggests an effective means for preventing the spread of disease through a population. Rather than selecting a group of random individuals from a population to vaccinate, it is much more effective to identify the friends of those individuals and vaccinate them.

Similar findings have been produced by other researchers looking at a variety of applications, such as the spread of computer viruses (Lloyd and May 2001) and the distribution of business intelligence in financial networks (Kadushin 1995). Generally speaking, research demonstrates that it takes a much smaller percentage of friends of members in a population to effect change than it does when relying on a group of randomly selected members.

Telephone or email chains or trees are commonly used by organizations to spread messages to their members, clients or prospects. Based on the findings discussed here, it would appear that the most efficient and effective means of disseminating information within a given population is to randomly select a group of individuals, have them identify a friend, and then ask those friends to transmit the message to their friends. To state this notion more formally, network transmission is superior to either the vastly more common hierarchical or sequential modes of distribution.

Strength and Creativity

Two more aspects of networks that merit our consideration are probably best expressed as paradoxical or, at least, counterintuitive notions—strength is a function of weakness and creativity is a collective rather than an individual activity.

In 1973, Mark Granovetter published a groundbreaking article called "The strength of weak ties." In it, he demonstrated that when networks are composed of strongly tied actors, such as would result from homophily and triadic closure, the network becomes cut off from outsiders and alternate viewpoints. New information and the ability to communicate outside of one's immediate environment then comes to rely on the handful of weak relationships that individual members of the network have with individual outsiders. These weak ties act as bridges or shortcuts to what is not known. In a related project (1974), he provided an example of job hunting. Those with whom we are strongly tied are likely to be aware of the same opportunities that we are. In order to hear about something different, we need access to a friend of a friend, unknown to us, and not part of our network.

In his initial study, Granovetter also suggested that a lack of weak ties could inhibit community development. When members of a community share religious, national, ethnic or social class identity, these factors tend to bind them strongly to one group, and segregate them from others, even when they live side-by-side with members of other well-defined groups. Energy expended in maintaining strong in-group ties, in the face of adversity, or the struggle for day-to-day existence, means that there is little energy, or will, available to pursue the sorts of weak ties outside the group that could potentially provide relief, or build a collective resource base through which to take action.

In *Bowling Alone* (2000), Robert Putnam suggests that a decline in social capital associated with the demise of opportunities to establish and maintain reciprocal ties has destroyed our communities and our civic engagement. Instead of participating in community activities, whether amateur sports or service organizations, we have individualized our leisure time, as we sit in front of our televisions. Further, Putnam is concerned that, as a consequence of internet technology: "Local heterogeneity may give way to more focused virtual homogeneity as communities coalesce across space" (178). We may not feel isolated, but we become insulated from alternate viewpoints and different ways of doing things. Ultimately, a lack of social diversity among our ties will lead to a decline in social cohesion. As Katherine Giuffre indicates, following Durkheim's notion of organic solidarity, it is multiple weak ties among dissimilar others that hold society together (2013: 200).

More recently, researchers have started to explore the reverse effect, expressed as the weakness of strong ties. Marton Karsai et al. (2014) found that strong ties inhibit the diffusion of information over time, because they confine the spreading process among individuals who engage in recurrent patterns of communication. Even though this type of research is in its very early stages, it certainly suggests the need for flexibility, openness and renewal in organizations.

The notion of weak ties, along with the idea of structural holes, can give us some interesting insights into the process of creativity. Even though we are likely to associate this process with gifted individuals, historical evidence and research on communities and enterprises like Apple (see Freiberger and Swaine 2000) has demonstrated that creativity is very much a collective undertaking. More specifically, Poppy McLeod et al. (1996) found that when people have exposure to others different from themselves, they are more likely to engage in divergent thinking, which is the key to innovation. The question that arises, then, becomes one of what sort of community or collectivity best supports this process.

Leading the charge on this matter is Richard Florida (2012), who thinks that members of the "creative class" are drawn to, or emerge out of, places that exhibit the things they value—openness, diversity and a vibrant street life, among other things. He envisions an eclecticism that arises out of weak ties among individuals, that is balanced with the existence of multiple small worlds (e.g., ethnic enclaves) to which individuals establish and maintain access through a series of bridging connections. Further, he suggests that creative individuals seek out venues that facilitate interaction with others. Ray Oldenburg (1989) referred to such locations as "third places," to differentiate them from home and work. The point of third places is nothing other than providing somewhere to hang out.

Network Governance

Bevir (2012) initially discusses network governance, along with hierarchical and market forms, under the heading of organizational governance. Networks differ from hierarchies in that they do not contain a central authority. They differ from markets because the members of a network engage in repeated and enduring exchanges that build trust and cooperation, rather than relying on a price mechanism. As a result, networks are viewed as being more egalitarian than the other two forms. The benefits to the organization are thought to be: a more efficient and reliable flow of information; the ability to cross jurisdictional and conceptual boundaries; ease in mobilizing resources, human and material; and the promotion and facilitation of change.

At the same time, the network form has been criticized for its lack of stability, which some might argue would encourage members to act opportunistically. Similarly, the complexity of networks would appear to make coordination and control very difficult, resulting in a counterintuitive inflexibility—on the assumption that change can only take place with the agreement of all members of the network. Perhaps most troubling, from a moral and political perspective, is the possibility that networks can disguise or eliminate lines of accountability. Well-connected individual actors or cabals with a vested interest in a particular outcome could potentially manipulate the network at the expense of the common good (see Mariolis and Jones 1982). In this sense, networks could be viewed as falling prey to the same downsides as more bureaucratic and hierarchical forms. The difference being—at least in theory—that with hierarchies there is a mechanism for control.

Further on, Bevir returns to networks when dealing with public governance. He suggests that, "the proliferation of networks was partly an unintended consequence of public sector reforms" (2012: 67). These reforms involved the marketization of services (contracting-out) and the empowerment of public service managers, resulting in a focus on finances and performance (managerialism), rather than the delivery of service. In response to these excesses, policies began to emphasize the formation of partnerships and the management of networks. The establishment of so-called public-private partnerships (see Hodge and Greve 2010) increased, with a focus on cooperation and co-production of both policies and services. This transition led to the need for network management, whereby the coordination and oversight of interdependent actors, based on trust and shared commitments, could compensate for the absence of central authority.

With respect to leadership within a network, Charles Kadushin points out that leaders tend to be those who can tolerate greater asymmetry in their relationships, which he euphemistically refers to as "unrequited love" (2012: 87). As he goes on to explain, leaders can be identified in terms of the extent to which they direct interaction toward others, rather than on the basis of how much attention is directed toward them. To put it more colloquially, leadership is about giving rather than receiving, and the action of giving does not come with the expectation of reciprocity.

Sustainability Governance

Rather than using the more common expression sustainable governance as the heading for this section—and, to be troublesome—sustainability governance was chosen to emphasize the fact that governance systems that are effective and good must be judged on the extent to which they support sustainability. In contrast, the notion of sustainable governance can be understood to imply that the objective is to establish a system of governance that can be sustained. While the latter goal may have merit, it only does so to the extent that the system of governance being sustained is one that facilitates the sustainability of the organization and beyond.

Introducing the concept of sustainability into the discussion raises a whole series of issues that, in parallel with debates about governance and leadership, are hotly contested by academics, politicians, special interest groups, the media and the public. For present purposes, however, three ways of thinking about sustainability will be highlighted. First, it involves a concern for what Freer Spreckley (1981) called the triple bottom line. Not only must organizations be concerned with their financial health, they must also balance those concerns with the expenditure of resources in support of social and environmental matters. It is not enough for organizations to take the position that they will not privilege financial wellbeing at the expense of social and environmental concerns; they must also operate in a manner that is constructive in these areas. I think it is fair to suggest that this approach was implicit in Hardin's discussions of understanding and developing solutions for the tragedy of the commons.

The second key aspect of sustainability is linked to Ashby's concept of requisite variety. In order for an organization to meet its targets with respect to all three elements just discussed, adequate resources must be allocated to alternate and potentially conflicting ways of doing business both inside and outside the organization. As already alluded to in discussing complex adaptive systems, the goal of acquiring requisite variety does not necessarily mean having more resources. Rather, it implies flexibility in both the type and arrangement of resources available to meet demands.

In this regard, Duit and Galaz (2008) identify three systems effects that governance must cope with. The first of these is threshold effects, abrupt and irreversible changes, often referred to "tipping points" (Gladwell 2001), that contrast with our expectations of the sort of smooth and gradual change we think we can control and cope with more effectively. Next, surprises can occur as a consequence of the interaction of various organizational components. These events are unpredictable with respect to their content, their timing and their consequences. Threshold effects and surprises sound similar, but the former refers to situations where incremental actions, that appear to be following a pattern, suddenly take off. Surprises are literally those things that seem to come out of nowhere. Finally, the notion of cascading refers to the fact that threshold effects and surprises can start a chain reaction of equally unpredictable and unintended consequences throughout an organization. Governance systems require a certain degree of flexibility in order to sustain the impact of such effects.

Third, the notion of capacity to act, central to understanding governance and leadership, can be viewed as an expression of sustainability. Poised systems, ones that are equipped to provide adequate information handling, decision-making and resource allocation, allow organizations to be sustainable.

Coupled with the concept of sustainability governance is the notion of good governance, which Bevir (2012) points out was initially equated with the existence of representative and responsible government. In the last few decades, this view has been modified to capture an emphasis on development, which is characterized by cooperation between various government and non-government organizations, as they attempt to achieve a shared global vision. Looking forward, Bevir suggests that good governance might best be thought of as collaborative governance, where all concerned parties come together to discuss, decide and implement plans for a better world. Further to this, good governance must be characterized by an explicit recognition of the ontological, epistemological, axiological and nomological foundations upon which it is based.

By way of offering organizations some practical advice, Bob Doppelt identifies the following five dominant characteristics of sustainable governance systems (2010: 253).

Follow a vision and inviolate set of principles focused on conserving the environment and enhancing socioeconomic wellbeing.

Continually produce and widely distribute information necessary for expanding the knowledge base and measuring progress toward the vision.

Engage all those affected by the activities of the organization.

Skillfully distribute the resources and equitably share the wealth generated by the organization.

Provide people with the freedom and authority to act within an agreed upon framework.

Even though he expresses these characteristics in terms of sustainable governance, it is clear that they directly address the governance of sustainability. They posit the need for establishing an overarching set of values, engaging in those activities that build capacity to act and maintaining flexibility built on the relationships among those involved.

From a somewhat more philosophical perspective, Dixon and Dogan suggest that a critical realist structurationist view of society leads to a set of eight governance propositions (2002: 190-91).

First, they suggest that there are no given or correct propositions about governance. Rather, there are only suppositions.

Second, governance problems cannot be solved; they can only be managed.

Third, the idea of good governance is not an objective standard; it is a contested and constructed terrain that achieves its relevance through ongoing discourse.

Fourth, the seeming instability of governance structures should be viewed as a strength and an opportunity, rather than as a threat.

Fifth, those who govern must seek to understand the intended meaning of arguments presented to them by various stakeholders through a diversity of perspectives.

Sixth, conflict is normal and all of those involved must come to accept the need for flexibility, balanced with the kind of restraint needed to ensure that conflict does not escalate, or become destructive.

Seventh, outcomes should be viewed in terms of sets of achievable goals, strategies that can be implemented and the acceptance of a tolerable level of conflict.

Eighth, and perhaps most importantly, the essence of good governance resides in the very fact that it remains a contested domain, constantly being renewed and reassessed.

11. Servant Leadership

Being a Servant First

Robert K. Greenleaf (1904-1990) worked in management development at AT&T for thirty-eight years, retiring early to establish the Center for Applied Ethics, now called the Greenleaf Center for Servant Leadership. He developed the idea of the servant leader in the late 1960s, based on his experience identifying and training future managers, and on his conviction that organizations exist for people, as much as people exist for the organization. Apart from his direct work experience, Greenleaf obtained much of the inspiration for his ideas from reading a short 1932 novel, *Journey to the East* (2003), by Nobel Prize-winning German author Hermann Hesse (1877-1962).

Servant leadership was a threshold concept for me primarily because of the refreshing and, in my opinion, right-minded view it offered. Furthermore, I found the fact that part of Greenleaf's inspiration arose out of his reading fiction—more specifically a work by Hermann Hesse—very appealing. I was a big fan of Hesse's novels in the 1970s and I had even entertained the idea of using his writings as the basis for my MA thesis, until I was rather forcefully dissuaded from doing so by my graduate supervisor, who thought that Hesse had little if anything of consequence to say about the human condition. Perhaps it was partially by way of vindication for this advice that I was attracted to Greenleaf's concept. However, while I was an avid reader of Hesse, I did not come to Greenleaf's ideas directly. Rather, I was introduced to them indirectly through a book by Max DePree called *Leadership is an Art* (1989).

Greenleaf originally presented his ideas about servant leadership in a 1969 essay that would become the first chapter of a 1977 book containing several more essays on the topic, specifically on the application of the concept in particular settings, such as business, education, boards of trustees and religious institutions. Even the original essay is composed of several small fragments that, if he were writing today, might have appeared as independent blog posts which, as he states at the outset, do not need to be read in any particular order.

The opening section of the essay, which serves as an introduction to the entries that follow, begins with a twofold acknowledgment. First, Greenleaf stresses his indebtedness to Hesse's novel as the source of the idea of the servant leader. Second, he explains that it took him more than a decade after reading the book to realize that it was calling him to rethink his views on contemporary prophecy.

The word prophecy literally means to say before hand—to foretell. In many cultures and religious traditions, the notion of prophecy is generally associated with the ability to interpret divine will and the duty to inform members of society of what their future will look like should they continue to behave in their current manner. Greenleaf suggests that there are many prophetic voices around today, as in the past, calling out for us to take action regarding some aspect or other of our collective social experience. The key for him, however, is not the absence or presence of prophecy, or even the particular message being conveyed by the prophet, but rather the extent to which there are seekers among the members of society who are willing to listen to and heed those voices. Seekers make prophets.

Greenleaf suggests that prophetic voices are calling us to "a personeity better able to live fully and serenely in these times"

(1977: 8). The term personeity was coined by the poet Samuel Taylor Coleridge (1772-1834), not as some literary neologism, but rather in an unpublished theological work in which he was developing an understanding of the doctrine of the Trinity (see Barth 1969). While our present concerns have little if anything to do with understanding the essence of the Christian God, the rarely used concept of personeity is extremely powerful in that it captures the ontological, epistemological and axiological aspects of the individual, in a single word. Greenleaf uses Coleridge's term, positing it as a human rather than divine attribute, to express his conviction that the realization of self is best captured in the extent to which the individual is other-directed. In other words, not only is the personal intertwined with the social, but the social must also take primacy over the personal in order for either to be fulfilled. The notion of personeity captures the fact that not only do prophets serve, but also that those who respond to prophets do so by serving. Causality, in this case, is a reciprocal process carried out among ontologically equivalent beings.

Living fully and serenely means stepping outside our comfort zone. In this regard, Greenleaf invokes the advice of the French absurdist philosopher Albert Camus (1913-1960), who, in his last published lecture, "Create Dangerously" (1960), called upon people to confront the exacting terms of our collective existence. As Greenleaf summarizes it:

> Accept the human condition, its suffering and its joys, and work with its imperfections as the foundation upon which individuals will build wholeness through adventurous creative achievement. (1977: 12)

In order to serve, individuals must both accept and create risk. Nothing is ever going to be perfect or complete, and the state of the world will always reflect a series of contradictions, controversies and seemingly insurmountable challenges.

Serving requires listening. It is common to conceive of leaders as those who tell others what to do and who tell them what things mean. Conversely, servants listen to what others have to say, to the ways that they understand what is going on around them, and to what they think needs to be done. Effective and productive listening requires more than just not speaking. It also requires a quieting of the mind and a genuine openness to others. We have a propensity to interpret silence as weakness, especially in those holding positions of authority. We find it awkward and disturbing, when in fact it may provide a great source of collective strength.

Related to the issues of listening and understanding is the notion of language. Greenleaf recognizes that the way we understand things not only reflects processes of construction through social interaction, but also the way in which we locate and associate new information with what we already know and have experienced. When we become trapped in a "closed verbal world," representing some objective or absolute understanding of some phenomenon, we lose the opportunity to serve and lead.

In a discussion that sounds remarkably similar to the idea of the Goldilocks effect, Greenleaf suggests that there are two types of people drawn to leadership. The first group thrives on the physical and emotional stress associated with the role, while the second endures the stresses in order to have the opportunity to lead. The third alternative, and one that is rarely observed, is the choice to perform in a manner that reflects a personal optimum, which he describes as "carrying an unused reserve of energy in all periods of normal demand so that one has the resilience to cope with the emergency" (19). This approach requires the ability to withdraw—taking time to rest and reorient oneself.

Greenleaf views foresight as the central ethic of leadership. For him, failing to foresee is an ethical failure. Fulfilling this moral obligation, however, requires a particular way of understanding time. The notion of now, rather than being equated with a static snapshot moment, is to be viewed as a moving organic unity of the past, present and future. By extension:

> Foresight means regarding the events of the instant moment
> and constantly comparing them with a series of projections

made in the past and at the same time projecting future events—with diminishing certainty as projected time runs out into the indefinite future. (26)

Parallel to his thoughts on listening, in order to practice foresight it is necessary for the individual to be aware of what is going on around them. Like listening, awareness is a difficult and disturbing skill to acquire. At the heart of this approach, is the need to see things as they are, rather than as we expect them to be.

Having extolled the virtues of conceiving of time as something that is continuous and flowing, rather than choppy and discrete, Greenleaf introduces an idea that may appear contradictory to this perspective. He suggests that accomplishing goals very often needs to take place one thing and one person at a time. Both of these aspects of incrementalism recognize, as captured in one of the tenets of symbolic interactionism, that people respond to things on the basis of the meaning that those things have for them. Movement takes place when people are ready to move. However, serving those involved can facilitate getting things in motion.

One of the last sections of Greenleaf's essay deals with the subject of enemies. He wants to know who is standing in the way of social progress and who is responsible for the mediocre performance of many of our major institutions. While acknowledging that the world does in fact contain stupid, lazy, evil and apathetic people, he does not place the blame on them. Rather he sees the situation this way.

> In short, the enemy is strong natural servants who have the potential to lead but do not lead, or who choose to follow a non-servant. They suffer. Society suffers. And so it may be in the future. (45)

He places the origin of this problem in the fact that most people will seek order—any kind of order—rather than live in chaos. Order, of course, manifests itself in the various systems we create, but Greenleaf views these structures as a product of human activity, not the source of it. As such, systems will come and go based on their usefulness in facilitating service.

To close out his essay, Greenleaf turns to an idea expressed by Leo, the central character (servant-leader) in Hesse's novel, about "the creations of poetry being more vivid and real than the poets themselves" (p. 47). What Greenleaf is drawing attention to with this reference is the idea that achieving true identity is at the same time a loss of identity. Serving, and therefore leading, is about being other-directed to the extent that you can only be known through the other.

Perhaps in an effort to establish some broader credibility for Greenleaf's ideas, especially among academics, and potentially in an effort to provide a conceptual basis for researching the model, Larry Spears (2010) suggests that servant leadership can be identified by ten characteristics: listening, empathy, healing, awareness, persuasion, conceptualization, foresight, stewardship, commitment to the growth of people and building community. For the most part, these characteristics correspond directly to the headings or content of the subsections of Greenleaf's essay. Dirk Van Dierendonck (2010) put together a similar list, identifying the six characteristics of servant leadership as: empowering and developing people, humility, authenticity, interpersonal acceptance, providing direction and stewardship. In contrast to Spears' list, this list demonstrates an effort to collect Greenleaf's major ideas into broader thematic areas, most of which have been discussed to some extent in the leadership literature. Aside from the fact that these lists can be viewed as highly reductionist, and an unnecessary step backward in terms of leadership theorizing, they reflect the prejudices of leadership research and the need, in order for it to be taken seriously, to articulate any theory in terms of measurable variables.

Despite its non-scholarly standing, the notion of servant leadership has recently found its way into some standard textbooks on leadership. Daft (2011) introduces the idea in his chapter on courage and moral leadership, as the next step along a continuum that begins with authoritarian management, and moves through participative management and stewardship, culminating in servant leadership, which he suggests can be identified by four basic precepts: put service before self-interest, listen first to affirm others, inspire trust by being trustworthy and nourish others and help them become whole (178). Similarly, Yukl (2013) introduces the concept in his chapter on ethical, servant, spiritual and authentic leadership. His coverage of the topic is rather cursory, and his main point appears to be that a limited amount of research has been carried out on the topic. He does, however, identify John Mackey, CEO and co-founder of Whole Foods, as an example of someone who has embraced the model in the actual practice of leadership (349).

Deborah Eicher-Catt offers an intriguing feminist critique of servant leadership (S-L), suggesting that it presents "a mythical theology of leadership for organizational life that upholds androcentric patriarchal norms" (2005: 17). Through a semiotic analysis of the gendered language and discourse of Greenleaf's essay, she suggests, among other things, that by placing the role of servant in apposition to that of leader, the model reinforces stereotypical notions of traditional female and male characteristics and behaviours. Further, she suggests that the model is politically motivated to appeal to women, as a refreshing and forward-thinking perspective on management, but also to appeal to senior management, almost exclusively male, who can further reinforce their dominance by showing their feminine side. Without going into too much detail, the following excerpt, which opens her conclusion, provides an illustrative example of her method and style.

> Organizational consultant, Ken Rhodes, claims that "servant-leadership is gender neutral because true service is genderless and true leadership is gender blind." If that were true, then we would see an increase of women in more responsible leadership positions and more men working in the service industry where S-L is the philosophy in use. (23)

It is difficult to determine from this passage whether Rhodes or Eicher-Catt is most guilty of employing faulty reasoning regarding correlation and causation, and of displaying a remarkable naïveté with respect to ideology and the human condition.

My reading suggests that Eicher-Catt bases much more of her critique of servant leadership on what others have said about it, than on what Greenleaf himself says in his essay. Additionally, her analysis appears to be focused more on demonstrating her virtuosity in exercising the tools of her trade (semiotics), than on attempting to understand and contextualize servant leadership. This is regrettable, as all ideas should be subjected to critical scrutiny. That is how we learn and that is how we make corrections. Perhaps, the best response to her review comes from Greenleaf himself.

> With education that is preponderantly abstract and analytical it is no wonder that there is a preoccupation with criticism and that not much thought is given to "What can I do about it?" (1977: 11)

By way of closing out this section, Greenleaf's idea of serving may provide a solution to Burns's paradox, which states that, if leadership and followership are so intertwined, is there is little value in differentiating between them (Burns 2003). For Burns, the key distinction is that leaders take initiative and thereby create a relationship. The received wisdom is that we spend most of our time as followers, when it is probably far more accurate, at least from an economic perspective, to say that we spend most of lives as employees, either formally or informally, in the service of others, in exchange for some kind of reward—whether it be love or money. However, we do not spend most of our lives as followers, any more than certain select individuals spend most of their lives as leaders. Just as leadership is highly transient, so is followership, both roles come into being simultaneously and disappear again once the situation that precipitated the emergence of leadership has passed. What remains constant is serving, whether through prophecy or in responding to it.

Leadership as an Art

Max DePree (b. 1924), former CEO of Herman Miller, a world-renowned furniture manufacturing company in Zeeland, Michigan, won the International Leadership Association's Lifetime Achievement Award in 2012. His 1989 book, *Leadership is an Art*, built on Greenleaf's concept of servant leadership and incorporating lessons from his own experience, is one of the finest and yet most underappreciated books ever produced on leadership. It is rarely cited by academics. As we have seen, much of what passes for scholarly research on leadership tells us much more about the researchers, and the restrictions they operate under, than it does about leadership. In contrast, DePree's book not only tells us a great deal about leadership, it also provides us with a superlative model of how to write about leadership.

Leadership is an Art consists of stories and anecdotes, which, as was the case with Greenleaf's original essay, can be read in any order. In a short time, readers come to see that DePree is an enthusiastic baseball fan and a jazz aficionado, but this fact should not be allowed to obscure or disqualify his insights. Earlier, I was critical of the construction of stories as they are presented in case studies, and especially of the way they were used by Kouzes and Posner. What makes DePree's stories different is the fact that he does not try to tell us what others are thinking or doing. Rather his stories are about how things strike him—what he has learned from observing what is going on around him.

At the core of DePree's book is an appreciation of the importance of the individual participant in any enterprise, and the way in which the relationships among individuals take precedence over structure. In terms of capacity to act, which he expresses as a new concept of work, the following individual rights are essential.

> 1. *The right to be needed.* The best chance for the needs of the group to be met are for the needs of individual members of the group to be met. In this regard, DePree asks whether you would "rather work as a part of an outstanding group or be part of a group of outstanding individuals" (29).

2. *The right to be involved.* This right consists of three elements. Input refers to ensuring a realistic opportunity for participation. Response refers to the obligation for engagement and interaction in all phases of goal accomplishment. Action is the translation of interaction into products and services.

3. *The right to a covenantal relationship.* The idea of a covenantal relationship is best understood in contrast to the more familiar contractual relationship. Contracts are legal documents, ratified by the signature of both parties, based on the premise that neither party can be trusted to uphold its end of the bargain. In contrast, a covenant has its foundation in trust that both parties intend to do what they have promised to do. It is a promise written on the heart, rather than on paper—a handshake rather than a signature.

4. *The right to understand.* Individuals need the opportunity to increase their competence through study and new experience. This involves knowing where you fit, what is expected of you, where the organization is going and, perhaps most importantly, why it is going there.

5. *The right to affect one's own destiny.* DePree speaks of personal dignity and the need for people to be involved and adequately informed of their career path within the organization, whether that means performance evaluation, promotion, transfer, training, reassignment or anything else.

6. *The right to be accountable.* The first thing to note about this is a right is that it is not expressed as an obligation. As with the distinction between contract and covenant, accountability is too often described in negative terms. By expressing more positively, the concept captures the idea of caring about what is going on in an organization and taking ownership.

7. *The right to appeal.* People not only need the opportunity to disagree, they need to know that they can do so in a supportive environment, without the fear of retribution.

8. *The right to make a commitment.* If people feel uncomfortable about the direction an organization is taking, or what their role in it is, they find it difficult to commit to being part of that organization. In this regard, I often speak to my students about "49-percenters," people who commit to meet you half way, but who stop just shy of that, forcing you to give a bit more in order compensate for the shortfall. Irrespective of the motivation for taking this approach, it prevents genuine interaction and the establishment of trust, thus impeding the building of capacity to act. We cannot wait and see. We need to commit.

Along with these rights, there are two concepts mentioned by DePree that merit special comment—entropy and literacy.

When giving a presentation to some financial analysts, during which he was asked a question about the most difficult thing he himself had to work on, he responded: "The interception of entropy" (110). Physicists tend to bristle at the co-opting of rigorous scientific concepts into other seemingly less precise and less objective realms of academic interest, whether as metaphors or as substantive concepts. After all, what could the second law of thermodynamics possibly have to do with leadership? Well, simply stated—things fall apart. Unless adequate energy is continually put into a system to maintain order, that system will increasingly move toward a state of disorder. DePree provides a list of twenty signs of entropy that people often fail to see. Here are a few:

A tendency toward superficiality.

A dark tension among key people.

No longer having time for celebration and ritual.

A growing feeling that rewards and goals are the same thing.

When problem-makers outnumber problem-solvers.

A loss of grace and style and civility.

The key point to pick up on here is that these signs of disorder are expressed in terms of interpersonal relationships.

One of DePree's most profound contributions is the idea of viewing personal maturity as a process best represented as "a continually rising level of literacy" (100).

Literacy levels are commonly used as a measure of human development and, for DePree, it is not just a question of more people being literate, but the idea that the individual must exert energy to become more literate—learning new things and learning new ways to learn. Literacy's opposite, illiteracy, is envisioned as a sure sign of economic and social underdevelopment, often associated with the oppression of women, and often the result of efforts to suppress opposition to a dominant ideology through a refusal to educate. What is rarely talked about, however, is aliteracy—the seemingly paradoxical situation where someone has the ability to read, but is not interested in doing so (see Agee 2005). Parallel to the way in which Greenleaf identified enemies, DePree appears to be saying that it is the aliterate rather than the illiterate individual that should be associated with increases in entropy. Literacy, and the maturity that comes from it, is not an epistemological problem as much as it is an axiological problem. Ignorance is a genuine social problem, but it can be dealt with through the provision of resources and opportunity—a technical fix. Apathy, on the other hand, is attitudinal and, as a consequence, can only be corrected through a fundamental shift in values—definitely not a technical fix.

One aspect of DePree's book that stands out, from the perspective of the book as artifact and learning aid, is the fact that it was produced with wide margins, an easy to read font and type size and wide line spacing. Cynics might suggest that, as short as the book already is, the spacious layout merely serves to puff up into book form what is really nothing more than an extended essay. After all, (substantial) books sell, but no one buys (mere) essays. Publishers, of course, hate white space—it's *expensive*. However, the real point of white space is that it is *expansive*, allowing for bounded but infinite flights of imagination and knowledge formation. Providing readers with a visual cue (space) for reading between the lines—surfing the interstitial spaces, as

Solway might express it—allows them to make their own connections and record them directly on the printed page.

As DePree states it: "Buying books is easy; owning them is not" (3). Part of that ownership is accomplished through interaction with the book, and the record of that interaction in the form of marginal notes helps the reader to remember what triggered a particular response, the content of that response and how it became incorporated into their body of knowledge.

The impact of these idiosyncratic notations, referred to as marginalia (see Jackson 2002), can be remarkable not just for the owner, but also for future readers. One of the most famous examples of this phenomenon is that of the French lawyer and amateur mathematician, Pierre de Fermat (1601-1665), who, in 1637, scribbled in the margins of his copy of the 3rd-century classic *Arithmetica*, by Diophantus of Alexandria, that he had discovered a solution for a particularly vexing problem in algebraic number theory, but that it was too long to write in the margin. Often dismissed as a hoax, generations of mathematicians tackled the problem, until a solution was finally found in 1995. This case also emphasizes the fact that, like Solway's idea of the anecdotal function, the thought that is triggered and the notes that are scribbled down may not appear to be related to the text with which they are associated. The important point is that reading a particular passage triggered something unpredictable and unintended. Having the opportunity (space) to write it down helps to ensure that it will not be lost.

Stretching this point a bit further, the combination of the original text along with the marginalia creates what is called a palimpsest. Despite the obscurity of the word, the concept is quite familiar and incredibly useful (see Carter 2012). One of the first big benefits of fax machines, for example, was that users could send a document back and forth, adding ever more layers of detail, corrections, questions and so on, to create a record of the development of shared understanding of an engineering drawing, an invoice or whatever else they could put down on paper. More recent versions of this exist in tools like track changes and comment bubbles in word processing software. Part of engaging in a continually rising level of literacy is to have the necessary tools to do so, and having white space, not just in books, but in every other structure we encounter, is essential to accomplishing that goal.

There is no simple way to sum up DePree's contribution and, in fact, trying to do so would be contrary to what he intended. What you get out of reading his book, as is true of any book for that matter, is a function of what you put into it. However, in an effort to steer the discussion back in the direction of leadership, the following quote seems appropriate.

> In a day when so much energy seems to be spent on maintenance and manuals, on bureaucracy and meaningless quantification, to be a leader is to enjoy the special privileges of complexity, of ambiguity, of diversity. (22)

As the stories in his book imply, and as has been stressed in various ways throughout this book, the challenges and opportunities associated with complexity, ambiguity and diversity reside in the relationships among those individuals participating in whatever enterprise it is that you are a part of. At the same time, as DePree recognizes, in order to do so "we need a lot of freedom, [but] there's no room for license" (50).

A New Way Forward

This closing section contains an exploration of one relatively recent effort to incorporate an alternative perspective on the nature and role of values in the practice of management, as presented by Gary Hamel in his book *What Matters Now* (2012). Part jeremiad, part pep-talk, chock full of clever one-liners, like, "If life had adhered to Six Sigma rules, we'd still be slime" (42), Hamel's book presents "a multi-faceted agenda for building organizations that can win in a world of relentless change, ferocious competition, and unstoppable innovation" (ix). The five things he thinks matter now are: values, innovation, adaptability, passion and ideology.

As a corrective to the recent and seemingly ongoing irresponsible and, many would argue, illegal activity on the part of some large corporations and financial institutions, Hamel calls for a "moral renaissance" in the way we do business. Incensed by the fact that the guilty parties have not been held accountable, he suggests that values matter now, more then they ever have.

Hamel observes that one consequence of the networked global economy is that products and strategies are easily copied, leading to fleeting successes and extreme difficulty in maintaining a competitive edge, let alone sustaining an enterprise for the long haul. His solution is for innovation to become an integral part of the normal day-to-day way we do business, rather than having it happen despite the systems we have in place. Related to innovation is the idea of adaptability. Organizations must learn to engage in constant strategic renewal, rather making changes in the face of some crisis or other. Perpetuating past ways of thinking and doing, for their own sake, is ultimately destructive.

Systemic innovation and the will to change require passion, which Hamel says emerges from a "righteous discontent with the status quo" (xi). Too many organizations are not only trapped in the past, but their atmosphere tends to quash or dampen enthusiasm and inspiration. It is not competence in organizations that is the problem, but rather a lack of ardor.

Finally, Hamel identifies the major stumbling block as the propensity for management to deify control. What is required is a shift in ideology—away from a concern for conformity and toward a focus on brilliance and uniqueness.

Hamel ends his book with a list of twenty-five so-called moonshots organized into six themes. As one might expect, the term moonshots is meant to capture the notion of aiming higher. The reason we have trouble doing so, as he sees it, is a lack of imagination. In one of his most colourful statements, he describes it this way.

> Like a zoo-born lion that knows only its cage, we can't imagine the sweet grasses and blue vistas of an organiza-

tional savannah where human beings are actually free to flourish. (244)

It is tempting to view his moonshots, however, as nostalgia for a time when the U.S. was actively engaged in the space race, and the success of the Apollo missions demonstrated just how much can be accomplished when the population of a country places its collective will behind reaching a single overarching goal. The six themes are: mending the soul, unleashing capabilities, fostering renewal, distributing power, seeking harmony and reshaping minds (246). All of these processes certainly appear to represent a more holistic and human centered approach to engaging in collective social enterprise, whether business or otherwise. The catch is that, in contrast to the dogged-determination and hard work carried out by NASA scientists to reach the moon, Hamel's themes amount to little more than timeless ideals—New Age platitudes—that no one knows how to translate into concrete action.

One of the things I did like about Hamel's book is the fact that, in advocating for a re-alignment of values through which we reclaim nobility, he cites Viktor Frankl's book, *Man's Search for Meaning* (1962). "For success, like happiness, cannot be pursued; it must ensue, and it only does so as the unintended consequence of one's personal dedication to a cause greater than oneself" (2012: 38). Frankl's book is an exploration of how a person can find meaning in the midst of extreme suffering, based on his first-hand experience as a prisoner in Nazi concentration camps—not a book that one would expect to be cited by a leading management guru, or to be found as required reading in business schools. Anecdotally, the same individual who dissuaded me from studying Hermann Hesse, introduced me to Frankl's book, along with a number of other books, like *The Plague* (1960) by Albert Camus, and Ernst Becker's *Denial of Death* (1973), all of which should be counted as obligatory reading, especially when it comes to understanding the primacy of values.

The main thing I did *not* like about Hamel's book, especially vivid in light of the Frankl quote, is his admission that he bet against the housing market and benefitted substantially from its demise.

> Indeed, in 2005 I bought a financial derivative from my broker that was, in effect, a bet against the housing market. The instrument was linked to a stock index that tracked the performance of America's largest home builders. For every 1 per cent decline in the value of the index, the value of my investment rose by 3 percent. The instrument expired in 2008 and paid off handsomely. My only regret is that I didn't bet bigger. (2013: 13)

For me, this admission betrays a bit too much of an acceptance of the free market, invisible hand, view of the situational ethics of capitalism, exacerbated with a hint of *Schadenfreude*. From my perspective, Hamel's statement comes dangerously close to undermining his entire program. Are his prescriptions only meant for others, while the genuinely astute (continue to) benefit at the expense of the noble?

12. Social Leadership

The time has come to spell out more clearly just what is meant by social leadership and to indicate what its value might be. The material presented in the previous chapters has meandered through topics that fall more generally under the category of leadership and those pertaining more directly to governance. In all of these discussions, the concepts of context, complexity, emergence, interaction and relationships have dominated the narrative. One final element that remains to be described in greater detail, however, is how we should understand the word social.

Privileging the Social

This section presents a brief survey of three initiatives that may be viewed as precursors to the idea of social leadership; their explicit use of the word social differentiates them from more traditional approaches in the areas they cover. While there may be other developments that some would consider antecedents to the idea of social leadership, the ones covered here are: corporate social responsibility, social marketing and social entrepreneurship.

Archie Carroll (1999) suggests that, even though the notion of corporate social responsibility (CSR) has a long and impressive history, Howard Bowen pioneered its emergence as a formal subject among academics and business leaders, in his 1953 book,

Social Responsibilities of the Businessman. While he did not use the term CSR, Bowen expressed the idea this way:

> It refers to the obligations of businessmen to pursue those policies, to make those decisions, or to follow those lines of action which are desirable in terms of the objectives and values of our society. (Cited in Carroll 1999: 270)

Building on this idea, Keith Davis (1960) suggested that taking a socially responsible approach to business would likely result in long-term economic gain. Davis is also well known for his "iron law of responsibility," which states that the social responsibility of a business leader should be commensurate with that leader's social power.

Since the 1970s, several alternate perspectives on CSR have emerged, reflecting a fundamental disagreement between two Nobel Prize-winning economists. As Davis (1973) pointed out, Milton Friedman (1912-2006) was of the opinion that for business leaders to accept any responsibility other than maximizing returns to their shareholders was an assault on freedom. In contrast, Paul Samuelson (1915-2009) thought that business leaders were obliged to extend their purview beyond mere financial gain. This tension continues to be at the heart of discussions of CSR and shows little sign of being resolved, in part because, as Abagail McWilliams and Donald Siegel (2000) demonstrate, the economic impact of CSR initiatives in most cases is neutral. As a consequence, business leaders have little motivation to allocate resources to activities that fail to provide them with a net gain.

More recently, in an effort to assess the state of our knowledge on the concept, as well as articulate a research agenda for the future, Herman Aguinis and Ante Glavas (2012) examined 588 journal articles and 102 books and book chapters on CSR. In their study, they adopt the following definition of CSR as: "context-specific organizational actions and policies that take into account stakeholders' expectations and the triple bottom line of economic, social, and environmental performance" (Aguinis 2011: 855). Among other things, these researchers found that "there seems to be a lack of understanding of the underlying mechanisms linking CSR with outcomes" (2012: 953). In other words, notwithstanding the best of intentions, we do not know how ideas get translated into action.

The term social marketing captures the idea that techniques developed in the marketing of products and services for financial gain can also be applied to the promotion of things that are good for society. Not to be confused with social media marketing, which employs social media as part of conventional (profit-driven) marketing campaigns, Philip Kottler and Gerald Zaltman (1971) originally conceived of the approach with reference to bringing about planned social change. Social marketing has been used extensively in a number of applications such as stop smoking campaigns, efforts to encourage people to get vaccinated against the flu, initiatives aimed at various aspects of developing a healthier lifestyle and the promotion of environmental stewardship (see Lee and Kotler 2011).

Marylyn Carrigan et al. (2011) examine whether it is possible for small local enterprises to influence broader societal change toward sustainability. They use the example of the "no plastic bag" campaign initiated by 43 retailers in the U.K. town of Modbury (pop. 1,500), which became the first plastic bag-free town in Europe in April 2007. A community social marketing campaign was established that included the distribution of 2,000 fair trade, recycled cotton bags, as well as a reliance on "catalytic individuals" to spread the message that what was good for the town was also good for business. The success of the program led to the inclusion of larger national and international retailers operating in the area, as well as expansion to several other towns in the U.K. Among their conclusions, the researchers suggest that a major reason initiating social change at the local level is so successful is that members are involved in the process and affected by the results in a more direct and personal manner.

In part a reflection of current global economic conditions, discussions of entrepreneurship have shifted from an emphasis on big business personalities (e.g., Richard Branson, Jeff Bezos, Howard

Schultz) to a focus on the large number of individuals involved in developing small and medium scale enterprises (SMEs) in local communities. Coupled with this is a shift away from viewing entrepreneurs as exceptional (rare) individuals, toward bringing out the entrepreneurial spirit in everyone (see Mehta 2012). Some of these individuals (e.g., Hugh Evans, Kerstin Forsberg, Sejal Hathi) are turning their efforts toward the delivery of social goods. In this regard, Samer Abu-Saifan proposes that:

> The social entrepreneur is a mission-driven individual who uses a set of entrepreneurial behaviours to deliver a social value to the less privileged, all through an entrepreneurially oriented entity that is financially independent, self-sufficient, and sustainable. (2012: 25)

A key aspect of this definition is the equation of the concept of an organization's mission with the delivery of social value to underprivileged or underserved constituencies. Abu-Saifan suggests that social entrepreneurial organizations operate either as non-profits with earned income strategies, or as for-profits with mission-driven strategies. In the former case, revenues and profits are used to further enhance social value delivery. In the latter, founders and investors may benefit financially from both the commercial and social activities of the organization.

Toyah Miller et al. (2012) set out to explore how compassion may give rise to social entrepreneurship. They suggest that compassion works as a motivator through "(1) increasing integrative thinking, (2) inducing pro-social judgments regarding the costs and benefits of social entrepreneurship, and (3) fostering commitment to alleviate others' suffering" (620). They go on to explain that, beyond compassion, the suggested course of action must be grounded in institutional support based on both pragmatic and moral legitimacy. The pragmatic aspect has to do with the demands placed on organizations by shareholders and others to demonstrate measurable performance in fulfilling social objectives along with financial ones. The moral aspect concerns growing disillusionment with the ability of traditional social service organizations to deliver public goods.

Viewing social entrepreneurship from the side of compassion and commitment has also been explored under the heading of venture capitalism (Letts et al. 1997). David Van Slyke and Harvey Newman (2006) present a case study of a community redevelopment initiative carried out by Tom Cousins in an area riddled with poverty, crime and lack of investment. They demonstrate that what differentiates venture philanthropy from more traditional forms of donating to public causes is the high level of commitment and direct involvement required on the part of the donor/investor.

In an effort to bring more academic rigor to discussions of social entrepreneurship, Roger Martin and Sally Osberg suggest that it involves

> forging a new, stable equilibrium that releases trapped potential or alleviates the suffering of the targeted group, and through imitation and the creation of a stable ecosystem around the new equilibrium ensuring a better future for the targeted group and even society at large. (2007: 35)

Despite efforts to introduce more formalism into discussions of social entrepreneurship—or perhaps because of them—the construct has been criticized for, among other things, its emphasis on exceptional individuals and the establishment of new organizational forms (see Zahra et al. 2009; Dacin et al. 2010). Certainly the centrality of notions like stability and equilibrium in the above definition sounds counter to the establishment of an ecosystem characterized by a relational ontology and constructivist epistemology, as advocated in these pages. However, the authors do identify a few points that are consistent with the social leadership framework.

First, the idea of trapped potential can be interpreted to reflect the stultifying effects of either too much agency (a commons) or too much structure (an anticommons). Second, the goal of alleviating the suffering of targeted groups could refer not just to poverty-based inequalities, but also to a broader range of social and environmental injustices. Third, even though individual initiatives will represent responses to particular circumstances in specific situations, the incremental building of a critical mass of effort and accomplishment will benefit society, more generally.

The recognition of the creation of social goods as a legitimate and, some would argue, priority goal of organizational activity has taken on many forms beyond the ones just discussed. For example, Michael Porter and Mark Kramer (2011) build on the notion of CSR to emphasize creating shared value (CSV). Their primary message is that it is not enough to accept responsibility—a decidedly passive response that need not translate into specific action. Instead, businesses must set out purposively to create social as well as economic value. In a more altruistic and ambitious vein, Muhammad Yunus (2009, 2011) advocates for the practice of social business, in which enterprises are created for the express purpose of addressing a social good—the primary example of which is the alleviation of global poverty. The sheer variety of initiatives can be interpreted in a positive light as reflecting the growing recognition of the importance of the social—and this is to be applauded. At the same time, however, the inability to establish adequate common ground not only serves to diminish effort through lack of focus, it also demonstrates, yet again, that axiological problems do not lend themselves to epistemological solutions—there is no technical fix. The way forward requires a realignment of values and courses of action that reflect those values. It also requires a more adequate recognition of the social dynamics that take place within organizations, irrespective of the goals they are attempting to accomplish.

Social Leadership

The objective of governance and leadership is to build capacity to act. While governance systems provide the environment in which activities are carried out, they also establish the conditions under which leadership can emerge. Consequently, they can be seen as reflecting a dual nature. First, they must possess an adequate degree of stability to allow for organizational continuity and in order to support action. Second, they must possess the flexibility required to respond to challenges and opportunities and to enable leadership to emerge when the circumstances and situation call for it. The necessary temporal permanence of governance systems can sometimes lead to the perception that, because so much effort has gone into establishing the system and the system has served the organization well in the past, structural permanence is also a necessity.

In contrast to the given-ness of governance, leadership is a transient phenomenon that comes and goes in an instant. Its occurrence may generate long-lasting effects, but attributing any degree of permanence to an act of leadership, or the person appearing to initiate it, results in the distribution of inadequate credit to those who respond and too much credit to the so-called leader, usually manifested in the form of disproportionate reward (promotion or fame) and continued expectation of performance. Even when conditions are right, leadership may not emerge. In order for that to occur, individuals must be poised to take advantage of the opportunity to lead, and others must be poised to respond to acts of leadership.

The idea of social leadership is meant to capture two critical assumptions about the way the world should work. First, as highlighted in the initiatives discussed above, collective social action must be directed toward the production of social goods, most broadly reflected under the rubric of sustainability. Any viable form of sustainability must, of course, reflect a balance among economic, environmental and social considerations established on the basis of shared axiological rather than epistemological assumptions. Second, as emphasized throughout the preceding chapters, the best way to maximize our potential in establishing capacity to act is by adopting a relational ontology (the privileging of collective engagement over individual action) and a constructivist/hermeneutic epistemology (the recognition of knowledge as what something means to those involved rather than what something means). The energy required to build capacity is social energy and, as reflected in the precepts of symbolic interactionism, the establishment and refinement of shared meaning through interaction with others is what generates that energy.

Some scholars have suggested that collective social action is the single most difficult thing in the world to accomplish (see Ostrom 2000). Part of the problem is related to the inappropriate foundational assumptions we make, or unknowingly live by, as we approach working with others. Similarly, the unnecessary and yet pervasive tension between order and disorder, structure and agency, anticommons and commons that typifies our efforts to balance predictability with freedom leaves us exhausted and unfulfilled. As Shannon Portillo (2012) demonstrates, rules can both facilitate and restrain behaviour. From a network perspective, as Mark Granovetter (1985) describes it, agency is socially embedded. Both of these scholars are pointing to the fact that the false dichotomies we have constructed do not reflect the way the world works. In order to facilitate capacity building, these dichotomies must be deconstructed.

In an effort to clarify the idea of capacity to act and the way in which structure and agency act together to constitute that capacity, the following diagrams may prove helpful. Figure three shows the three possible ways in which structure and agency can be related to one another. The top arrangement (1) assumes that these phenomena are binary. On this assumption, each aspect would repel the other—they could not co-exist. The middle arrangement (2) pictures them along a continuum. The social state of any given situation or circumstance could be plotted along this continuum in a way that reflects how much of each component is contributing to the current state. In this case, the total could only be 100 per cent. If a particular situation resulted from 63 per cent agency, then structure could only contribute 37 per cent, and vice-versa. The arrangement on the bottom (3) places structure and agency in an orthogonal relationship allowing for a greatly expanded realm of contributory influence. For example, a situation may reflect only a 10 per cent contribution from both structure and agency, thus representing a gross underutilization of resources in the construction of capacity. Similarly, a situation could arise in which a large percentage of both elements come together to produce what we might think of as an almost 200 per cent effort.

1. Ⓢ Ⓐ

2.   S ⟵———⟶ A

3.   S $\llcorner$

    A

Figure Three

Taking this representation to the next level, with the horizontal axis assigned to represent structure and the vertical axis representing agency, it is possible to illustrate some alternate governance arrangements and how they impact capacity to act. Following the standard logic of graphs, moving further to the right on the horizontal axis would represent an increase in structure (rules). Similarly, moving up along the vertical axis would represent an increase in agency. Figure four shows a line (curve) extending from an interception point a short distance up the agency axis and extending along the structure axis, moving ever closer to the axis as it goes. This figure represents those situations where people perceive structure to be the primary driving force of action, such as in a bureaucracy. Potential capacity to act is considered to be equal to the area under the curve, as represented by the shading.

There are two critical observations to make about Figure four. First, the fact that the curve approaches the axis as it moves to the right reflects what Weber referred to as the "iron cage of bureaucracy"—the situation of being so trapped by rules that the capacity to do anything at all, for all intents and purposes, disappears. Second, the area under the curve represents the maximum possible capacity to act—one that in actual practice is never attained. As an extension of these two properties, it is easy to see that any effort to increase capacity, solely by increasing structure, is impeded by diminishing returns. Twice as many rules do not double capacity.

Figure five demonstrates the complementary situation in which structure is limited and agency is allowed to increase. As was the case with increasing structure, increasing agency only marginally increases capacity. Similarly, any efforts to greatly increase individual freedom of action does so at the expense of what little structure was there in the first place.

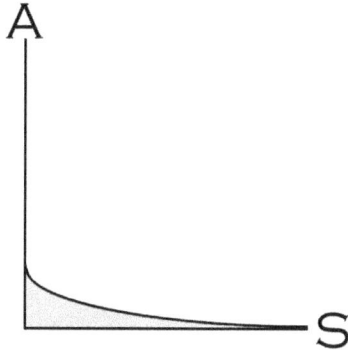

Figure Four

While both of the previous examples allow for some mixture of the two factors, they represent extreme cases that, while there are undoubtedly examples of such organizations, do not provide for the optimal, let alone maximal, construction of capacity to act. Allowing for the fact that actual organizations reflect a broad range of possibilities,

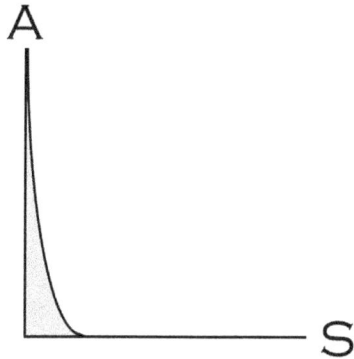

Figure Five

Figure six illustrates what we might think of as a general-purpose representation of capacity to act. The curves from the previous two graphs have been combined into one continuous curve encompassing the full range of possibilities, or interaction space, for structure and agency. The shaded region near the origin represents what is likely to be the actual boundary of potential capacity to act

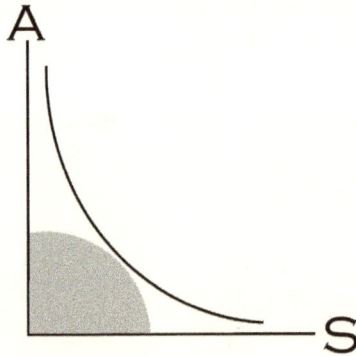

Figure Six

for most organizations. Various checks and balances, either in the form of rules (e.g., contracts, regulatory constraints) or personal behaviour (e.g., management, intransigence), are the primary mechanisms that prevent or discourage operating at extremes.

Borrowing a term from physics—more specifically, the theory of general relativity—the curve in the Figure six can be viewed as an event horizon. The notion captures the fact that activities taking place beyond that horizon, in space or time, can have no impact upon the observer (see Stannard 2008). For our purposes, the term captures the notion that the amount of agency or structure available to build capacity is limited to what falls under the curve. In order to expand capacity, the boundary must be extended, and that requires energy—energy in the form of organization, energy that comes from interaction. Figure seven illustrates a shift in the event horizon away from the origin associated with an expanded capacity to act. While an organization is unlikely to need to utilize its entire capacity to act on a long-term or sustained basis, failure to continue putting energy into maintaining an expanded event horizon (entropy) will render the organization incapable of responding to a crisis or opportunity when such a situation does occur.

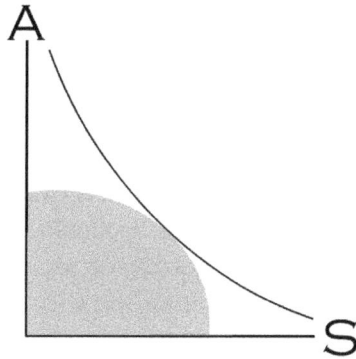

Figure Seven

Social interaction is a relational process of organizing (creating order) that leads to intersubjective accomplishment (see Prus 1996). This accomplishment amounts to shared understanding which informs action and which continues to evolve as individuals collectively encounter ever-changing situations and circumstances. These statements may sound trite or simplistic; we may be of the opinion that we are engaging in social interaction all the time. However, as Boris Groysberg and Michael Slind (2012) point out, fully engaging in conversation requires intention, not just with respect to outcome, but also with respect to appreciation of those with whom you are conversing. It also requires discipline, part of which is related to being quiet—not just keeping your mouth shut, but quieting the mind.

We have become so accustomed to a noisy world, that our ability to be quiet has all but vanished. In fact, it is likely that for many people, the few moments of genuine quiet they experience induce as much, if not more, anxiety than the normal cacophony to which they are exposed. We are barraged with so much visual, sonic and tactile data that our overloaded senses shut down out of exhaustion. On those rare occasions when we are immersed in quiet, we fidget and fuss, searching for distraction—no longer knowing how to cope. Applying this notion more broadly, I would suggest that the current problems we are encountering with our systems of governance and leadership are best viewed as crises of noise.

Communications experts speak about the signal-to-noise ratio of a transmission. What this concept expresses is the extent to which the meaningful and intentional part of a message can win out against the interference that it encounters. Advances in information and communications technologies have provided media gurus, politicians, marketers and special interest groups with the means to flood the environment with noise. Some of this effort, of course, is designed to drown out the competition—a futile exercise that results in nothing but escalation. Some of it, however, is designed to prevent discussion, the sort of discussion that would lead to understanding and, beyond that, to evaluation, condemnation and the initiation of alternative courses of action. In the absence of quiet, and in order for social interaction to be constructive, individuals must learn to filter out noise. This is a difficult challenge but, as Nate Silver (2012) so aptly demonstrated with respect to predicting performance in baseball, it can be done.

Max DePree equated maturity with a rising level of literacy. Consistent with the philosophical position advocated in this book, literacy is constructed through interaction with others—it is relational. By the same token, immaturity can be viewed not as illiteracy, but as aliteracy. We know how to interact with others and we are eminently equipped to do so. We fail to mature when we choose *not* to interact. We succumb to the noise. Building capacity to act requires filtering out the noise. It is a question of intentionality—an expression of shared values.

ooooo

By way of closing out this book, I would like to return to the idea of threshold concepts and offer three propositions that I hope are both troublesome and useful. First, while I recognize that the word "leader" is unlikely to be stricken from the vocabulary of business, politics and other realms of public activity, I would ask that you disassociate it from the concept of leadership. Restrict your use of the word leader solely to express position. As a corollary to this suggestion, bring the concept of management back into your vocabulary, not just as an expression of position, but also as a set of attitudes, skills and knowledge that serves an essential function in the day-to-day operation of every social enterprise.

Second, adopt a foundational approach to understanding what is going on around you. Start ferreting out the hidden, misunderstood and deliberately distorted ontological, epistemological, axiological and nomological assumptions made by the people you encounter in all aspects of your life. Most importantly, learn to identify those ontological and epistemological proclamations that are substituted for value statements in an effort to disguise antisocial or asocial actions.

Finally, start to build capacity to act through conversation—one person at a time. Do so by listening, paying attention, being aware and then contributing. That is the essence of social leadership. It is a process and a prescription. And, of course, this process must take place within a particular context—one that is constantly being constructed and altered, as circumstances dictate. That is governance.

At the risk of simplification and reductionism—and inconsistent with the philosophical position advocated throughout these pages—I feel compelled to offer a succinct statement about what social leadership is, if for no other reason than to provide readers with a conversation starter. Social leadership encompasses the process of building capacity through the confluence of opportunity, preparedness and right intention.

References

Abbott, Andrew. 1988. *The System of Professions*. Chicago: University of Chicago Press.

Abell, Ellen, and Simons, Shoshana. 2000. How much can you bend before you break: An experience of using constructionist consulting as a tool for organizational learning in the corporate world. *European Journal of Work and Organizational Psychology* 9(2): 159-75.

Abu-Saifan, Samer. 2012. Social entrepreneurship: Definition and boundaries. *Technology Innovation Management Review* (February): 22-27.

Adler, Paul S., and Borys, Bryan. 1996. Two types of bureaucracy: Enabling and coercive. *Administrative Science Quarterly* 41(1): 61-89.

Agee, Jim. 2005. Literacy, aliteracy, and lifelong learning. *New Library World* 106(5/6): 244-52.

Aquinis, Herman. 2011. Organizational responsibility: Doing good and doing well. In S. Zedeck (ed.), *APA Handbook of Industrial and Organizational Psychology, Vol. 3*, 855-79. Washington: American Psychological Association.

Aguinis, Herman, and Glavas, Ante. 2012. What we know and don't know about corporate social responsibility: A review and research agenda. *Journal of Management* 38(4): 932-68.

Andersen, Susan M., and Chen, Serena. 2002. The relational self: An interpersonal socio-cognitive theory. *Psychological Review* 109(4): 619-45.

Anderson, Philip. 1999. Complexity theory and organizational science. *Organization Science* 10(3): 216-32.

Ashby, W. Ross. 2011. Variety, constraint, and the law of requisite variety. *Emergence: Complexity and Organization* 13(1-2): 190-207.

Asmuss, Birte, and Svennevig, Jan. 2009. Meeting talk: An introduction. *Journal of Business Communication* 46(1): 3-22.

Atkinson, J. Maxwell. 1982. Understanding formality: Notes on the categorization and production of "formal" interaction. *British Journal of Sociology* 33(1): 86-117.

Auyang, Sunny Y. 1998. *Foundations of Complex System Theories*. Cambridge: Cambridge University Press.

Baert, Patrick. 1998. *Social Theory in the Twentieth Century*. Cambridge: Polity Press.

Balkundi, Prasad, and Kilduff, Martin. 2005. The ties that lead: A social network approach to leadership. *Leadership Quarterly* 16(6): 941-61.

Barnard, Chester I. 1938. *The Functions of the Executive*. Cambridge: Harvard University Press.

Barth, J. Robert. 1987. *Coleridge and Christian Doctrine*. New York: Fordham University Press.

Bass, Bernard M., and Avolio, Bruce J. 1990. *Multifactor Leadership Questionnaire*. Palo Alto: Consulting Psychologists Press.

Bass, Bernard M., and Avolio, Bruce J. 1994. *Improving Organizational Effectiveness through Transformational Leadership*. Thousand Oaks: Sage.

Basurto, Xavier, and Ostrom, Elinor. 2013. The core challenges of moving beyond Garrett Hardin. *Journal of Natural Resources Policy Research* 1(3): 255-59.

Bathurst, Ralph, Jackson, Brad, and Statler, Matt. 2010. Leading aesthetically in uncertain times. *Leadership* 6(3): 311-30.

Becker, Ernst. 1973. *Denial of Death*. New York: Free Press.

Bennis, Warren G. 1989. *Why Leaders Can't Lead: The Unconscious Conspiracy Continues*. San Francisco: Jossey Bass.

Bentham, Jeremy. 1823. *An Introduction to the Principles of Morals and Legislation*. London: Pickering and Wilson.

Berger, Peter L., and Luckmann, Thomas. 1967. *The Social Construction of Reality*. New York: Doubleday.

Bevir, Mark. 2012. *Governance: A Very Short Introduction*. Oxford: Oxford University Press.

Blackburn, Simon. 2001. *Ethics: A Very Short Introduction*. Oxford: Oxford University Press.

Blumer, Herbert. 1969. *Symbolic Interactionism*. Berkeley: University of California Press.

Boden, Deirdre. 1994. *The Business of Talk: Organizations in Action*. Cambridge: Polity.

Bohm, David. 1980. *Wholeness and the Implicate Order*. London: Routledge and Kegan Paul.

Boushey, Heather. 2012. Growing from the middle out: U.S. jobs and the economy in Obama's second term. *Public Policy Research* 19(3): 181-87.

Bowen, Howard R. 1953. *Social Responsibilities of the Businessman*. New York: Harper and Row.

Bradbury, Hilary, and Lichtenstein, Benyamin. 2000. Relationality in organizational research: Exploring the "space between." *Organizational Science* 11(5): 551-64.

Branson, Richard. 2011. *Losing My Virginity: How I Survived, Had Fun, and Made a Fortune Doing Business My Way*. London: Virgin.

Brinkhurst, Marena. 2010. In the shadow of the anticommons: The paradox of overlapping exclusion rights and open-access resource degradation in India's wastelands. *Journal of Economic Issues* 44(1): 139-62.

Brook, Daniel. 2001. The ongoing tragedy of the commons. *Social Science Journal* 38(4): 611-16.

Brown, Douglas J., and Keeping, Lisa M. 2005. Elaborating the construct of transformational leadership: The role of affect. *Leadership Quarterly* 16(2): 245-72.

Buchanan, James M., and Yoon, Yong J. 2000. Symmetric tragedies: Commons and anticommons. *Journal of Law and Economics* 43(1): 1-14.

Burk, Dan L., and Lemley, Mark A. 2009. *The Patent Crisis and How the Courts Can Solve It*. Chicago: University of Chicago Press.

Burns, James M. 1978. *Leadership*. New York: Harper and Row.

Burns, James M. 2003. *Transforming Leadership: A New Pursuit of Leadership*. New York: Atlantic Monthly Books.

Burt, Ronald S. 1992. *Structural Holes: The Social Structure of Competition*. Cambridge: Harvard University Press.

Burt, Ronald S. 2004. Structural holes and good ideas. *American Journal of Sociology* 110(2): 349-99.

Caldarelli, Guido, and Catanzano, Michele. 2012. *Networks: A Very Short Introduction*. Oxford: Oxford University Press.

Campbell, Robert A. 2010. Why the fair use doctrine should be eliminated. *Society* 47(4): 322-27.

Camus, Albert. 1960. Create dangerously. *Resistance, Rebellion, and Death*, 249-72. New York: Alfred A. Knopf.

Camus, Albert. 1960. *The Plague*. London: Penguin.

Capra, Fritjof. 1975. *The Tao of Physics*. Boston: Shambhala.

Capra, Fritjof. 1983. *The Turning Point: Science, Society and Rising Culture*. New York: Bantam.

Carrigan, Marylyn, Moraes, Caroline, and Leek, Sheena. 2011. Fostering responsible communities: A community social marketing approach to sustainable living. *Journal of Business Ethics* 100(3): 515-34.

Carroll, Archie. 1999. Corporate social responsibility: Evolution of a definitional construct. *Business & Society* 38(3): 268-95.

Carter, Pam. 2012. Policy as palimpsest. *Policy and Politics* 40(3): 423-43.

Carver, John, and Carver, Miriam. 1996. *Basic Principles of Policy Governance*. San Francisco: Jossey Bass.

Carver, John, and Carver, Miriam. 2006. *Reinventing Your Board: A Step-by-Step Guide to Implementing Policy Governance*, 2nd ed. San Francisco: Wiley.

Christakis, Nicholas, A. and Fowler, James H. 2010. Social network sensors for early detection of contagious outbreaks. *PloS One* 5(9): e12948.

Christensen, C. Roland, and Hansen, Abby J. 1987. *Teaching and the Case Method*. Boston: Harvard Business School.

Collins, Jim. 2001. *Good to Great*. New York: Harper Business.

Cournot, Augustin. 1963. *Researches into the Mathematical Principles of the Theory of Wealth: With Irving Fisher's Original Notes*. Homewood: Richard D. Irwin.

Covey, Stephen R. 1989. *The 7 Habits of Highly Effective People: Powerful Lessons in Personal Change*. New York: Simon & Schuster.

Craig, Gary. 2007. Community capacity building: Something old, something new…? *Critical Social Policy* 27(3): 335-59.

Cunliffe, Ann L., and Eriksen, Matthew. 2011. Relational leadership. *Human Relations* 64(11): 1425-49.

Dacin, Peter A., Dacin, M. Tina, and Matear, Margaret. 2010. Social entrepreneurship: Why we don't need a new theory and how we move forward from here. *Academy of Management Perspectives* 24(3): 37-57.

Daft, Richard L. 2011. *The Leadership Experience*, 5th ed. Mason: South-Western Cengage Learning.

Davenport, Thomas H., and Kim, Jinho. 2013. *Keeping Up With the Quants*. Boston: Harvard Business Review Press.

Davis, Keith. 1960. Can business afford to ignore social responsibilities? *California Management Review* 2(3): 70-6.

Davis, Keith. 1973. The case for and against business assumption of social responsibilities. *Academy of Management Journal* 16(2): 312-22.

Dawkins, Richard. 1976. *The Selfish Gene*. Oxford: Oxford University Press.

Deal, Terrence E., and Kennedy, Allan A. 2000. *Corporate Cultures: The Rites and Rituals of Corporate Life*. Cambridge: Da Capo Press.

De Bono, Edward. 1971. *Practical Thinking*. London: Cape.

Deppermann, Arnulf, Schmitt, Reinhold, and Mondada, Lorenza. 2010. Agenda and emergence: Contingent and planned activities in a meeting. *Journal of Pragmatics* 42(6): 1700-18.

DePree, Max. 1989. *Leadership is an Art*. New York: Dell.

Dewey, John, and Bentley, Arthur F. 1949. *Knowing the Known*. Boston: Beacon Press.

DiMaggio, Paul J., and Powell, Walter W. 1983. The iron cage revisited: Institutional isomorphism and collective rationality in organizational fields. *American Sociological Review* 48: 147-60.

Dixon, John, and Dogan, Rhys. 2002. Hierarchies, networks and markets: Responses to societal governance failure. *Administrative Theory and Practice* 24(1): 175-96.

Dobbin, Frank. 2009. *Inventing Equal Opportunity*. Princeton: Princeton University Press.

Donnelly, James H., Gibson, James L., and Ivancevich, John M. 1971. *Fundamentals of Management*. Austin: Business Publications.

Doppelt, Bob. 2010. *Leading Change Toward Sustainability*, 2nd ed. Sheffield: Greenleaf.

Dorfman, Peter W. 2003. International and cross-cultural leadership research. In *Handbook for International Management Research*, B. J. Punnett and O. Shenkar (eds.), 267-349. Ann Arbor: University of Michigan Press.

Drath, Wilfred H. 2001. *The Deep Blue Sea: Rethinking the Source of Leadership*. San Francisco: Jossey Bass.

Drucker, Peter F. 1959. *Landmarks of Tomorrow*. New York: Harper & Row.

Drucker, Peter F. 1973. *Management: Tasks, Responsibilities, Practices*. New York: Harper and Row.

Drucker, Peter F. 1992. *The Age of Discontinuity: Guidelines to Our Changing Society*, 2nd ed. Piscataway: Transaction.

Drucker, Peter F. 1999. *Management Challenges for the 21st Century*. New York: Harper Collins.

Duit, Andreas, and Galaz, Victor. 2008. Governance and complexity: Emerging issues for governance theory. *Governance* 21(3): 311-35.

Eicher-Catt, Deborah. 2005. The myth of servant leadership: A feminist perspective. *Women and Language* 28(1): 17-25.

Eisenhardt, Kathleen M. 1989. Agency theory: An assessment and review. *Academy of Management Review* 14(1): 57-74.

Elias, Norbert. 1978. *What is Sociology?* New York: Columbia University Press.

Elliott, Douglas J., and Baily, Martin N. 2009. *Telling the Narrative of the Financial Crisis: Not Just a Housing Bubble*. Washington: Brookings Institution.

Emirbayer, Mustafa. 1997. Manifesto for a relational sociology. *American Journal of Sociology* 103(2): 281-317.

Emirbayer, Mustafa, and Mische, Ann. 1998. What is agency? *American Journal of Sociology* 103(4): 962-1023.

Epstein, Marc J. 2008. *Making Sustainability Work*. San Francisco: Berrett-Koehler.

Erakovic, Liljana, and Jackson, Brad. 2009. Promoting leadership in governance and governance in leadership: Establishing a research agenda. *Proceedings of the 13th Asian and Pacific Region Organization Studies Conference, Monterey, Mexico*.

Faust, Katherine. 2010. A puzzle concerning triads in social networks: Graph constraints and the triad census. *Social Networks* 32: 221-33.

Fayol, Henri. 1949. *General and Industrial Management.* London: Pitman.

Feld, Scott L. 1991. Why your friends have more friends than you do. *American Journal of Sociology* 96(6): 1464-77.

Fiese, Barbara H., and Schwartz, Marlene. 2008. *Reclaiming the Family Table: Mealtimes and Child Health and Wellbeing.* Ann Arbor: Society for Research in Child Development.

Fletcher, Joseph. 1966. *Situation Ethics.* Philadelphia: Westminster.

Florida, Richard. 2012. *The Rise of the Creative Class, Revisited.* New York: Basic Books.

Follett, Mary P. 1924. *Creative Experience.* New York: Longmans, Green.

Ford, Jackie, and Harding, Nancy. 2007. Move over management we are all leaders now. *Management Learning* 38(5): 475-93.

Foucault, Michel. 1972. *The Archaeology of Knowledge.* New York: Pantheon.

Foucault, Michel. 1977. *Discipline and Punish: The Birth of the Prison.* London: Allen Lane.

Frankl, Viktor. 1962. *Man's Search for Meaning.* Boston: Beacon Press.

Freiberger, Paul, and Swaine, Michael. 2000. *Fire in the Valley: The Making of the Personal Computer,* 2nd ed. New York: McGraw-Hill.

Fulcher, James, 2004. *Capitalism: A Very Short Introduction.* Oxford: Oxford University Press.

Gardner, John W. 1990. *On Leadership.* New York: Free Press.

Garen, John E. 1994. Executive compensation and principal-agent theory. *Journal of Political Economy* 102(6): 1175-99.

Garfinkel, Harold. 1967. *Studies in Ethnomethodology.* Englewood Cliffs: Prentice-Hall.

Geddes, Patrick. 1915. *Cities in Evolution.* London: Williams.

Gerstner, Charlotte R., and Day, David V. 1997. Meta-analytic review of leader-member exchange theory: Correlates and construct issues. *Journal of Applied Psychology* 82(6): 827-44.

Giddens, Anthony. 1984. *The Constitution of Society.* Cambridge: Polity.

Gini, Al, and Marcoux, Alexei M. 2012. *The Ethics of Business: A Concise Introduction.* Lanham: Rowan and Littlefield.

Giuffre, Katherine. 2013. *Communities and Networks.* Cambridge: Polity.

Gladwell, Malcolm. 2002. *The Tipping Point.* New York: Back Bay Books.

Gleick, James. 2008. *Chaos: Making a New Science,* rev. ed. New York: Penguin.

Glover, Dominic. 2010. The corporate shaping of GM crops as a technology for the poor. *Journal of Peasant Studies* 37(1): 67-90.

Goffman, Erving. 1961. *Asylums.* New York: Doubleday.

Goffman, Erving. 1967. *Interaction Ritual: Essays on Face-to-Face Behavior.* New York: Pantheon.

Goleman, Daniel. 2004. *Primal Leadership: Realizing the Power of Emotional Intelligence.* Boston: Harvard Business School Press.

Gouldner, Alvin W. 1954. *Patterns of Industrial Bureaucracy.* Glencoe: Free Press.

Granovetter, Mark. 1973. The strength of weak ties. *American Journal of Sociology* 78(6): 1360-80.

Granovetter, Mark. 1985. Economic action and social structure: The problem of embeddedness. *American Journal of Sociology* 91(3): 481-510.

Greenleaf, Robert K. 1977. *Servant Leadership: A Journey into the Nature of Legitimate Power and Greatness.* New York: Paulist Press.

Greenleaf, Robert K., and Spears, Larry C. 2002. *Servant Leadership: A Journey into the Nature of Legitimate Power and Greatness, 25th Anniversary Edition.* New York: Paulist Press.

Grint, Keith. 2005. *Leadership: Limits and Possibilities.* New York: Palgrave Macmillan.

Groysberg, Boris, and Slind, Michael. 2012. *Talk, Inc.* Boston: Harvard Business Review Press.

Guare, John. 1990. *Six Degrees of Separation.* New York: Vintage.

Guthey, Eric, Clark, Timothy, and Jackson, Brad. 2009. *Demystifying Business Celebrity.* London: Routledge.

Hall, Edward T., and Hall, Mildred R. 1990. *Understanding Cultural Differences.* Yarmouth: Intercultural Press.

Hambrick, Donald C. 2007. Upper echelons theory: An update. *Academy of Management Review* 32(2): 334-43.

Hamel, Gary. 2012. *What Matters Now*. San Francisco: Jossey Bass.

Hanak, Irmi. 1998. Chairing meetings: Turn and topic control in development communication in rural Zanzibar. *Discourse and Society* 9(1): 33-56.

Hansen, Hans, Ropo, Arja, and Sauer, Erika. 2007. Aesthetic leadership. *Leadership Quarterly* 18(6): 544-560.

Haque, Umair. 2011. *The New Capitalist Manifesto*. Boston: Harvard Business School Publications.

Hardin, Garrett. 1968. The tragedy of the commons. *Science* 162: 1243-48.

Harris, Zellig S. 1952. *Discourse analysis*. Language 28(1): 1-30.

Harter, Nathan. 2006. *Clearings in the Forest: On the Study of Leadership*. West Lafayette: Purdue University Press.

Haslam, S. Alexander, and Ryan, Michelle K. 2008. The road to the glass cliff: Differences in the perceived suitability of men and women for leadership position in succeeding and failing organizations. *Leadership Quarterly* 19(5): 530-46.

Heifetz, Ronald A. 1994. *Leadership without Easy Answers*. Cambridge: Harvard University Press.

Heller, Michael A. 1998. The tragedy of the anticommons: Property in the transition from Marx to markets. *Harvard Law Review* 111(3): 621-88.

Heller, Michael A. 2008. *The Gridlock Economy: How Too Much Ownership Wrecks Markets, Stops Innovation, and Costs Lives*. New York: Basic Books.

Heller, Michael A. 2013. The tragedy of the anticommons: A concise introduction and lexicon. *Modern Law Review* 76(1): 6-25.

Heller, Michael A., and Eisenberg, Rebecca S. 1998. Can patents deter innovation? The anticommons in biomedical research. *Science* 280(5364): 698-701.

Hernandez, Morela, Eberly, Marion B., Avolio, Bruce J., and Johnson, Michael D. 2011. The loci and mechanisms of leadership: Exploring a more comprehensive view of leadership theory. *Leadership Quarterly* 22(6): 1165-85.

Hersey, Paul, and Blanchard, Kenneth H. 1967. *Management of Organizational Behavior*. Englewood Cliffs: Prentice-Hall.

Hesse, Hermann. 2003. *Journey to the East*. New York: Picador.

Hitt, Michael A., Middlemist, R. Dennis, and Mathis, Robert L. 1986. *Management: Concepts and Effective Practice*. Saint Paul: West Publishing.

Hobbes, Thomas. 2008. *Leviathan*. Oxford: Oxford Paperbacks.

Hodge, Graeme, and Greve, Carsten. 2010. Public-private partnerships: Governance scheme of language game? *Australian Journal of Public Administration* 69(S1): S8-S22.

Hodson, Randy, Martin, Andrew W., Lopez, Steven H., and Roscigno, Vincent J. 2012. Rules don't apply: Kafka's insights on bureaucracy. *Organization* 20(2): 256-78.

Hofstede, Geert. 1980. *Culture's Consequences: International Differences in Work-Related Values*. Thousand Oaks: Sage.

Hogg, Michael A. 2001. A social identity theory of leadership. *Personality and Social Psychology Review* 5(3): 184-200.

Hollander, Edwin P. 1978. *Leadership Dynamics: A Practical Guide to Effective Relationships*. New York: Free Press.

Holmes, Janet, and Marra, Meredith. 2004. Leadership and managing conflict in meetings. *Pragmatics* 14(4): 439-62.

Hosking, David M. 2000. Ecology in mind, mindful practices. *European Journal of Work and Organizational Psychology* 9(2): 147-58.

Hough, Alan. 2002. *The Policy Governance Model: A Critical Examination. Working Paper No. 6*. Brisbane: Centre for Philanthropy and Nonprofit Studies.

House, Robert J., Hanges, Paul, Javidan, Mansour, Dorfman, Peter W., and Gupta, Vipin. 2004. *Culture, Leadership and Organizations: The GLOBE Study of 62 Societies*. Thousand Oaks: Sage.

Howell, Jane M., and Shamir, Boas. 2005. The role of followers in the charismatic leadership process: Relationships and their consequences. *Academy of Management Review* 30(1): 96-112.

Huber, Bernard. 2009. *Negotiating the Political Ecology of Aboriginal Resource Management: How Mi'kmaq Manage their Moose and Lobster Harvest in Unama'ki, Nova Scotia, Canada*. Unpublished M.Sc. thesis. Wellington: Victoria University.

Huisman, Marjan. 2001. Decision-making in meetings as talk-in-interaction. *International Journal of Management and Organization* 31(3): 69-90.

Hunter, Samuel T., Bedell-Avers, Katrina E., and Mumford, Michael D. 2007. The typical leadership study: Assumptions, implications, and potential remedies. *Leadership Quarterly* 18(5): 435-46.

Jackson, Brad, and Parry, Ken. 2011. *A Very Short, Fairly Interesting and Reasonably Cheap Book about Studying Leadership*, 2nd ed. Thousand Oaks: Sage.

Jackson, Heather J. 2002. *Marginalia: Readers Writing in Books*. New Haven: Yale University Press.

Johns, Gary. 2006. The essential impact of context on organizational behavior. *Academy of Management Review* 31(2): 386-408.

Jonason, Peter K., Slomski, Sarah, and Partyka, Jamie. 2012. The dark triad at work: How toxic employees get their way. *Personality and Individual Differences* 52(3): 449-53.

Kadushin, Charles. 1995. Friendship among the French financial elite. *American Sociological Review* 60(2): 202-21.

Kadushin, Charles. 2012. *Understanding Social Networks: Theories, Concepts, and Findings*. Oxford: Oxford University Press.

Kafka, Franz. 1968. *The Trial*. New York: Schocken Books.

Kafka, Franz. 1998. *The Castle*. New York: Schocken Books.

Kaplan, Allan. 2000. Capacity building: Shifting the paradigms of practice. *Development in Practice* 10(3/4): 517-26.

Karsai, Marton, Perra, Nicola, and Vespignani, Alessandro. 2014. Time varying networks and the weakness of strong ties. *Scientific Reports* 4(4001): 1-6.

Katz, Daniel, and Kahn, Robert L. 1978. *The Social Psychology of Organizations*. New York: John Wiley and Sons.

Kauffman, Stuart A. 1991. Antichaos and adaptation. *Scientific American* 265(2): 78-84.

Kellerman, Barbara. 2004. *Bad Leadership*. Boston: Harvard Business Press.

Kenny, Sue, and Clarke, Matthew. 2012 *Challenging Capacity Building: Comparative Perspectives*. Basingstoke: Palgrave Macmillan.

Kernis, Michael H. 2003. Toward a conceptualization of optimal self-esteem. *Psychological Inquiry* 14(1): 1-26.

Kipling, Rudyard. 1902. *Just So Stories*. London: Macmillan.

Kjaer, Anne M. 2004. *Governance*. Cambridge: Polity Press.

Kosnik, Lea R. 2010. *From Cournot to Commons: An Analysis of Regulatory Property Rights*. SSRN Working Paper, http://www.ssrn.com.

Kosnik, Lea R. 2012. The anticommons and the environment. *Journal of Environmental Management* 101: 206-17.

Kottler, Philip, and Zaltman, Gerald. 1971. Social marketing: An approach to planned social change. *Journal of Marketing* 35(1): 3-12.

Kouzes, James, and Posner, Barry. 2007. *The Leadership Challenge*, 4th ed. San Francisco: Jossey Bass.

Kouzes, James, and Posner, Barry. 2012. *The Leadership Challenge*, 5th ed. San Francisco: Jossey Bass.

Kuhn, Thomas. 1970. *The Structure of Scientific Revolutions*. Chicago: University of Chicago Press.

Ladkin, Donna. 2008. Leading beautifully: How mastery, congruence and purpose create the aesthetic of embodied leadership practice. *Leadership Quarterly* 19(1): 31-41.

Ladkin, Donna. 2010. *Rethinking Leadership: A New Look at Old Leadership Questions*. Cheltenham: Edward Elgar.

Lazarsfeld, Paul F., and Merton, Robert K. 1954. Friendship as a social process: A substantive and methodological analysis. *Freedom and Control in Modern Society* 18(1): 18-66.

Lee, Nancy R., and Kotler, Philip. 2011. *Social Marketing: Influencing Behaviors for Good*, 4th ed. Thousand Oaks: Sage.

Leffler, Melvyn P. 2013. Defense on a diet: How budget crises have improved U.S. strategy. *Foreign Affairs* 92(6): 65-76.

Lencione, Patrick M. 2004. *Death by Meeting: A Leadership Fable*. San Francisco: Jossey Bass.

Letts, Christine, Ryan, William, and Grossman, Allen. 1997. Virtuous capital: What foundations can learn from venture capitalists. *Harvard Business Review* 75(2): 36-44.

Liang, Neng, and Wang, Jiaqian. 2004. Implicit mental models in teaching cases: An empirical study of popular MBA cases in the US and China. *Academy of Management Learning and Education* 3(4): 397-413.

Lloyd, Alun L., and May, Robert M. 2001. How viruses spread among computers and people. *Science* 292(5520): 1316-17.

Lloyd, William F. 1833. *Two Lectures on the Checks to Population*. Oxford: Oxford University Press.

Lovejoy, Arthur O. 1960. *The Great Chain of Being*. New York: Harper and Row.

Lu, Yong. 2009. The social organization of a criminal hacker network: A case study. *International Journal of Information Security and Privacy* 3(2): 90-104.

Lucas, Ursula, and Mladenovic, Rosina. 2006. Developing new world views: Threshold concepts in introductory accounting. In Meyer, Jan H. F., and Land, Ray. (eds.) *Overcoming Barriers to Student Understanding: Threshold Concepts and Troublesome Knowledge*, 148-59. New York: Routledge.

Maccoby, Michael. 2000. Narcissistic leaders: The incredible pros, the inevitable cons. *Harvard Business Review* 78(1): 68-77.

Machiavelli, Niccolo. 1958. *The Prince*. New York: Dutton.

Maines, David R. 1982. In search of mesostructure in the negotiated order. *Journal of Contemporary Ethnography* 11(3): 267-79.

Mallin, Chris. 2009. *Corporate Governance*. Oxford: Oxford University Press.

Malthus, Thomas R. 1798. *An Essay on the Principle of Population*. Oxford: Oxford University Press.

Mariolis, Peter, and Jones, Maria H. 1982. Centrality in corporate interlock networks: Reliability and stability. *Administrative Science Quarterly* 27(4): 571-85.

Martin, Roger L., and Osberg, Sally. 2007. Social entrepreneurship: The case for definition. *Stanford Social Innovation Review* 5(2): 28-39.

Marx, Karl. 1930. *Capital*. New York: Dutton.

Maxwell, John C. 1998. *The 21 Irrefutable Laws of Leadership*. New York: Thomas Nelson.

Mayntz, Renate. 1993. Governing failures and the problem of governability: Some comments on a theoretical paradigm. In Kooiman, J. (ed.) *Modern Governance: New Government—Society Interactions*, 9-20. London: Sage.

Mayo, Elton. 1945. *The Social Problems of an Industrial Civilization*. Boston: Harvard University.

McLean, Bethany, and Elkind, Peter. 2003. *The Smartest Guys in the Room: The Amazing Rise and Scandalous Fall of Enron*. New York: Portfolio.

McLeod, Poppy L., Lobel, Sharon A., and Cox, Taylor H. 1996. Ethnic diversity and creativity in small groups. *Small Group Research* 27(2): 248-64.

McWilliams, Abagail, and Siegel, Donald. 2000. Corporate social responsibility and financial performance: Correlation or mis-specification. *Strategic Management Journal* 21(5): 603-09.

Meek, V. Lynn. 1988. Organizational culture: Origins and weaknesses. *Organization Studies* 9(4): 453-73.

Mehta, Monica. 2012. *The Entrepreneurial Instinct*. New York: McGraw-Hill.

Meindl, James R. 1995. The romance of leadership as a follower-centric theory: A social constructionist approach. *Leadership Quarterly* 6(3): 329-41.

Meindl, James R., Ehrlich, Sanford B., and Dukerich, Janet M. 1985. The romance of leadership. *Administrative Science Quarterly* 30(1): 78-102.

Mesny, Anne. 2013. Taking stock of the century-long utilization of the case method in management education. *Canadian Journal of Administrative Sciences* 30(1): 58-66.

Meyer, Jan H. F., and Land, Ray. 2003. Threshold concepts and troublesome knowledge (1): Linkages to ways of thinking and practicing. In Rust, C. (ed.) *Improving Students Learning: Theory and Practice: Ten Years On*, 412-24. Oxford: Oxford Centre for Staff and Learning Development, Oxford Brookes University.

Meyer, Joanna M. 2012. The real error in *Citizens United*. *Washington and Lee Law Review* 69: 2171-231.

Milgram, Stanley. 1967. The small world problem. *Psychology Today* 1: 62-7.

Miller, Toyah L., Grimes, Matthew G., McMullen, Jeffery S, and Vogus, Timothy J. 2012. Venturing for others with heart and head: How compassion encourages social entrepreneurship. *Academy of Management Review* 37(4): 616-40.

Minkler, Meredith. 2012. *Community Organizing and Community Building for Health and Welfare*. New Brunswick: Rutgers University Press.

Mintzberg, Henry. 1973. *The Nature of Managerial Work*. New York: Harper & Row.

Murray, Vic. 1997. Three booklets and three books on nonprofit boards and governance. *Nonprofit Management and Leadership* 7(4): 439-45.

Murrell, Kenneth L. 1997. Emergent theories of leadership for the next century: Towards relational concepts. *Organizational Development Journal* 15(3): 35-42.

Murthy, Dhiraj. 2013. *Twitter: Social Communication in the Twitter Age*. Cambridge: Polity.

Neale, Jenny. 2001. Against the odds: Combining family and the leadership role. In K. W. Perry (ed.), *Leadership in the Antipodes: Findings, Implications and a Leader Profile*, 141-65. Wellington: Institute of Policy Studies and the Centre for the Study of Leadership.

Nechansky, Helmut. 2008. Elements of a cybernetic epistemology: Decisions, control and principles of societal organization. *Kybernetes* 37(1): 83-93.

Nielsen, Mie Femo. 2013. Stepping stones in opening and closing department meetings. *Journal of Business Communication* 50(1): 34-67.

Nobbie, Patricia D., and Brudney, Jeffrey L. 2003. Testing the implementation, board performance, and organizational effectiveness of the policy governance model in nonprofit boards of directors. *Nonprofit and Voluntary Sector Quarterly* 32(4): 571-95.

Nooteboom, Bart. 2006. Simmel's treatise on the triad (1908). 2006. *Journal of Institutional Economics* 2(3): 365-83.

North, Douglass C. 1990. *Institutions, Institutional Change and Economic Performance*. Cambridge: Cambridge University Press.

Offermann, Lynn R., Kennedy, John K., and Wirtz, Philip W. 1994. Implicit leadership theories: Content, structure and generalizability. *Leadership Quarterly* 5(1): 43-58.

Oldenburg, Ray. 1989. *The Great Good Place*. New York: Paragon.

Ostrander, Susan A. 2012. Agency and initiative by community associations in relations of shared governance: Between civil society and local state. *Community Development Journal* 48(4): 511-24.

Ostrom, Elinor. 2000. Collective action and the evolution of social norms. *Journal of Economic Perspectives* 14(3): 137-58.

Padgett, John F., and Ansell, Christopher K. 1993. Robust action and the rise of the Medici, 1400-1434. *American Journal of Sociology* 98(6): 1259-1319.

Parisi, F., and Depoorter, B. 2003. Fair use and copyright protection: A price theory explanation. *International Review of Law and Economics* 21(4): 453-73.

Pearce, Craig L., and Conger, Jay A. 2003. *Shared Leadership: Reframing the Hows and Whys of Leadership.* Thousand Oaks: Sage.

Pelzer, Peter. 2002. Disgust and organization. *Human Relations* 55(7): 841-60.

Peter, Laurence J., and Hull, Raymond. 1969. *The Peter Principle: Why Things Always Go Wrong.* New York: William Morrow.

Peters, Thomas J., and Waterman, Robert H. 1982. *In Search of Excellence: Lessons from America's Best-Run Companies.* New York: Harper and Row.

Pfeffer, Jeffrey, and Salancik, Gerald R. 1978. *The External Control of Organizations: A Resource Dependence Perspective.* New York: Harper and Row.

Pizzorno, Alessandro. 1991. On the individualistic theory of social order. In *Social Theory for a Changing Society*, edited by Pierre Bourdieu and James S. Coleman. Boulder: Westview, pp. 209-31.

Porter, Lyman W., and McLaughlin, Grace B. 2006. Leadership and the organizational context: Like the weather? *Leadership Quarterly* 17(6): 559-76.

Porter, Michael E., and Kramer, Mark. 2011. Creating shared value. *Harvard Business Review* 89(1/2): 62-77.

Porterfield, Sally F., Polette, Keith, and French Baulim, Tita. 2009. *Perpetual Adolescence: Jungian Analyses of American Media, Literature, and Pop Culture.* Albany: SUNY Press.

Portillo, Shannon. 2012. The paradox of rules: Rules as resources and constraints. *Administration and Society* 44(1): 87-108.

Prus, Robert C. 1996. *Symbolic Interaction and Ethnographic Research: Intersubjectivity and the Study of Human Lived Experience.* Albany: SUNY Press.

Putnam, Robert D. 2000. *Bowling Alone: The Collapse and Revival of American Community.* New York: Simon & Schuster.

Raelin, Joseph. 2003. *Creating Leaderful Organizations*. San Francisco: Berrett-Koehler.

Riordan, Michael, and Hoddeson, Lillian. 1997. *Crystal Fire: The Birth of the Information Age*. New York: Norton.

Robert, Henry M. III, Honemann, Daniel H., & Balch, Thomas J. 2011. *Robert's Rules of Order Newly Revised*, 11th ed. Cambridge: Da Capo.

Robin, Marie-Monique. 2010. *The World According to Monsanto*. New York: New Press.

Rogelberg, Steven G., Scott, Clifton W., Agypt, Brett, Williams, Jason, Kello, John E., McCausland, Tracy, and Olien, Jessie L. 2013. Lateness to meetings: Examination of an unexplored temporal phenomenon. *European Journal of Work and Organizational Psychology* (ahead-of-print): 1-19.

Rose, Carol. 1986. The comedy of the commons: Custom, commerce, and inherently public property. *University of Chicago Law Review* 53(3): 711-81.

Rosser, J. Barkley. 1999. On the complexities of complex economic dynamics. *Journal of Economic Perspectives* 13(4): 169-92.

Rost, Joseph C. 1995. Leadership: A discussion about ethics. *Business Ethics Quarterly* 5(1): 129-42.

Sacks, Harvey, Schegloff, Emanuel A., and Jefferson, Gail. 1974. A simplest systematics for the organization of turn-taking for conversation. *Language* 50(4): 696-735.

Sayles, Leonard R. 1964. *Managerial Behavior: Administration in Complex Organizations*. New York: McGraw-Hill.

Schein, Edgar H. 2010. *Organizational Culture and Leadership*, 4th ed. San Francisco: Jossey Bass.

Schneider, Marguerite, and Somers, Mark. 2006. Organizations as complex adaptive systems: Implications of complexity theory for leadership research. *Leadership Quarterly* 17(4): 351-65.

Schwartzman, Helen B. 1989. *The Meeting: Gatherings in Organizations and Communities*. New York: Plenum.

Scott, W. Richard, and Davis, Gerald F. 2007. *Organizations and Organizing: Rational, Natural, and Open System Perspectives*. Upper Saddle River: Pearson Prentice Hall.

Selznick, Philip. 1952. *The Organizational Weapon*. New York: McGraw-Hill.

Shamir, Boas. 2007. From passive recipients to active co-producers. In *Follower-Centered Perspectives on Leadership*, edited by B. Shamir, R. Pillai, M.C. Bligh, and M. Uhl-Bien, ix-xxxix. Greenwich: Information Age Publishing.

Shannon, Claude E. 1948. A mathematical theory of communication. *The Bell Systems Journal* 27: 379-423; 623-56.

Silver, Nate. 2012. *The Signal and The Noise: Why So Many Predictions Fail but Some Don't*. New York: Penguin.

Simmel, Georg. 1971. *On Individuality and Social Forms*. Chicago: University of Chicago Press.

Sinclair, Amanda. 2007. *Leadership for the Disillusioned*. Crows Nest: Allen & Unwin.

Smith, Adam. 1964. *The Wealth of Nations*. New York: Dutton.

Solway, David. 1991. The anecdotal function: A reconsideration of education lost. *Interchange* 22(4): 77-87.

Solway, David. 1997. *Lying about the Wolf*. Montreal: McGill-Queen's University Press.

Spears, Larry C. 2010. Character and servant leadership: Ten characteristics of effective, caring leaders. *Journal of Virtues & Leadership* 1(1): 25-30.

Spreckley, Freer. 1981. *Social Audit: A Management Tool for Co-operative Working*. Leeds: Beechwood College.

Stanford, Geoffrey. 1977. *Bourinot's Rules of Order*, 3rd rev. ed. Toronto: McLelland and Stewart.

Stannard, Russell. 2008. *Relativity: A Very Short Introduction*. Oxford: Oxford University Press.

Stehr, Nico. 1994. *Knowledge Societies*. Thousand Oaks: Sage.

Stewart, Rosemary. 1982. *Choices for the Manager: A Guide to Understanding Managerial Work*. Englewood Cliffs: Prentice Hall.

Stiglitz, Joseph E. 2003. *Globalization and Its Discontents*. New York: Norton.

Stout, Margaret. 2012a. Competing ontologies: A primer for public administration. *Public Administration Review* 72(3): 388-98.

Stout, Margaret. 2012b. Toward a relational language of process. *Administrative Theory & Praxis* 34(3): 407-32.

Sun Tzu. 2002. *The Art of War*. London: Dover.

Susskind, Lawrence E., and Cruikshank, Jeffrey L. 2006. *Breaking Robert's Rules*. New York: Oxford University Press.

Taylor, Frederick W. 1911. *The Principles of Scientific Management*. New York: Harper.

Thomas, David, and Inkson, Kerr. 2004. *Cultural Intelligence*. San Francisco: Berrett-Koehler.

Tourish, Dennis, and Vatcha, Naheed. 2005. Charismatic leadership and corporate cultism at Enron: The elimination of dissent, the promotion of conformity and organizational collapse. *Leadership* 1(4): 455-80.

Turkle, Sherry. 2012. *Alone Together: Why We Expect More from Technology and Less from Each Other*. New York: Basic Books.

Uhl-Bien, Mary. 2006. Relational leadership theory: Exploring the social processes of leadership and organizing. *Leadership Quarterly* 17(6): 654-76.

Uhl-Bien, Mary, Marion, Russ, and McKelvey, Bill. 2007. Complexity leadership theory: Shifting leadership from the industrial age to the knowledge era. *Leadership Quarterly* 18(4): 298-318.

Urbaniak, Tom. 2011. *Action, Accommodation, Accountability: Rules of Order for Canadian Organizations*. Duncan: Writing on Stone Press.

Van Dierendonck, Dirk. 2010. Servant leadership: A review and synthesis. *Journal of Management* 20(10): 1-34.

Van Slyke, David M., and Newman, Harvey K. 2006. Venture philanthropy and social entrepreneurship in Community redevelopment. *Nonprofit Management and Leadership* 16(3): 345-68.

Vanneste, Sven, Van Hiel, Alain, Parisi, Francesco, and Depoorter, Ben. 2006. From tragedy to disaster: Welfare effects of commons and anticommons dilemmas. *International Review of Law and Economics* 26(1): 104-22.

Wallison, Peter J. 2011. Three narratives about the financial crisis. *Cato Journal* 31(3): 535-49.

Warner, Malcolm. 2007. Kafka, Weber and organization theory. *Human Relations* 60(7): 1019-38.

Watts, Duncan J. 2003. *Six Degrees: The Science of a Connected* Age. New York: W. W. Norton.

Weick, Karl E. 1969. *The Social Psychology of Organizing*. Reading: Addison-Wesley.

Wenger, Etienne. 1998. *Communities of Practice*. Cambridge: Cambridge University Press.

Wenger, Etienne, McDermott, Richard, and Snyder, Willam M. 2002. *Cultivating Communities of Practice*. Boston: Harvard Business School Press.

Whitehead, Alfred N. 1948. *Science and the Modern World*. New York: Mentor.

Whitehead, Alfred N. 1967. *Adventures of Ideas*. New York: Free Press.

Wilbur, Janice R., Wilbur, Michael, Garrett, Michael T., and Yuhas, Meredith. 2001. Talking circles: Listen, or your tongue will make you deaf. *Journal for Specialists in Group Work* 26(4): 368-84.

Williams, Cindy. 2013. Accepting austerity: The right way to cut defense. *Foreign Affairs* 92(6): 54-64.

Wilson, James Q. 1988. *Bureaucracy*. New York: Basic Books.

Yip, Jeffrey, and Raelin, Joseph A. 2011. Threshold concepts and modalities for teaching leadership practice. *Management Learning* 43(3): 333-54.

Young, Michael. 1958. *The Rise of the Meritocracy, 1870-2033: An Essay on Education and Inequality*. London: Thames & Hudson.

Yukl, Gary. 2012. Effective leadership behavior: What we know and what questions need more attention. *Academy of Management Perspectives* 26(4): 66-85.

Yukl, Gary. 2013. *Leadership in Organizations*, 8th ed. Upper Saddle River: Pearson.

Yunus, Muhammad. 2009. *Creating a World without Poverty*. New York: PublicAffairs.

Yunus, Muhammad. 2011. *Building Social Business*. New York: PublicAffairs.

Zahra, Shaker A., Gedajlovic, Eric, Neubaum, Donald O., and Shulman, Joel M. 2009. A typology of social entrepreneurs: Motives, search processes and ethical challenges. *Journal of Business Venturing* 24(5): 519-32.

Zhang, Haina, Cone, Malcolm H., Everett, Andre M., and Elkin, Graham. 2011. Aesthetic leadership in Chinese business: A philosophical perspective. *Journal of Business Ethics* 101(3): 475-91.

Ziedonis, Rosemarie H. 2004. Don't fence me in: Fragmented markets for technology and patent acquisition strategies of firms. *Management Science* 50(6): 804-20.

Žižek, Slavoj. 2004. What Rumsfeld doesn't know that he knows about Abu Ghraib. *In These Times* (May 21).

Index

www.ingramcontent.com/pod-product-compliance
Lightning Source LLC
Chambersburg PA
CBHW021555210326
41599CB00010B/461